Introducing Erlang
Getting Started in Functional Programming

Simon St.Laurent

Beijing · Boston · Farnham · Sebastopol · Tokyo

Introducing Erlang

by Simon St.Laurent

Printed in the United States of America.

Published by O'Reilly Media, Inc., 1005 Gravenstein Highway North, Sebastopol, CA 95472.

O'Reilly books may be purchased for educational, business, or sales promotional use. Online editions are also available for most titles (*http://oreilly.com/safari*). For more information, contact our corporate/institutional sales department: 800-998-9938 or *corporate@oreilly.com*.

Editor: Dawn Schanafelt
Production Editor: Colleen Lobner
Copyeditor: Christina Edwards
Indexer: WordCo Indexing Services
Interior Designer: David Futato
Cover Designer: Karen Montgomery
Illustrator: Rebecca Demarest

March 2017:   Second Edition

Revision History for the Second Edition
2017-02-28:   First Release

See *http://oreilly.com/catalog/errata.csp?isbn=9781491973370* for release details.

978-1-491-97337-0

[LSI]

Table of Contents

Preface

Erlang has long been a mysterious dark corner of the programming universe, visited mostly by developers who need extreme reliability or scalability and people who want to stretch their brains.

Developed at Ericsson to serve on telephone-switching equipment, it seemed like a strangely special-purpose language until recently, when our computer and network architectures came to look a lot more like massively parallel telephone-switching equipment. Thanks to the spread of NoSQL data stores CouchDB and Riak, you may already be using Erlang without realizing it, and Erlang is moving out into many more fields. WhatsApp is a classic Erlang success story.

Erlang provides a short path from discipline to resilience. The decisions made by the creators of the language let the Erlang environment seamlessly scale and handle failure in ways that other environments have to manage by adding ever more infrastructure. In my utterly biased opinion, any application that needs to run for a long time and scale to many interactions should be built in Erlang (or its more recent cousin Elixir).

If you come from pretty much any background other than functional programming, exploring Erlang will require you to clear your mind of many of the techniques used in other programming languages. Forget classes, forget variables that change values—even forget the conventions of variable assignment.

Instead, you're going to have to think about pattern matching, message passing, and establishing pathways for data rather than telling it where to go. Erlang programming can feel like making a key whose teeth set the tumblers on a lock just right for the key to pass, or playing pachinko and watching the balls fall through a maze.

Sound strange? It is—but also enjoyable, powerful, and fun.

My first explorations of Erlang confused me and excited me at the same time. I'd had some experience with what I'd called "invariant variables," variables that can be bound to a value only once, in XSLT. That created a lot of headaches for me until I realized I was coming at the problems all wrong, and then it suddenly made sense.

Who This Book Is For

This book is mostly for people who've been programming in other languages but want to look around. Maybe you're being very practical, and Erlang's distributed model and the resulting scale and resilience advantages appeal to you. Maybe you want to see what this "functional programming" stuff is all about. Or maybe you're just going for a hike, taking your mind to a new place.

I suspect that functional programming is more approachable as a first language, before you've learned to program in other paradigms. However, getting started in Erlang—sometimes even just installing it—requires a fair amount of computing skill. If you're a complete newcomer to programming, welcome, but there will be a few challenges along the way.

Who This Book Is Not For

This book is not for people in a hurry to get things done.

If you already know Erlang, you don't likely need this book unless you're looking for a slow brush-up.

If you're already familiar with functional languages, you may find the pacing of this "Gentle Introduction" hopelessly slow. Definitely feel free to jump to another book that moves faster if you get bored. Come back if you find the others go too fast, and feel welcome to use this as a companion guide or reference with other books.

What This Book Will Do For You

In his book *Seven Languages in Seven Weeks*, Bruce Tate suggests that "Erlang makes hard things easy and easy things hard." This book will get you through the "easy things hard" part, and show you a bit of the promised land of "hard things easy."

In practical terms, you'll learn to write simple Erlang programs. You'll understand why Erlang makes it easier to build resilient programs that can scale up and down with ease. Perhaps most importantly, you'll be able to read other Erlang resources that assume a fair amount of experience and make sense of them.

In more theoretical terms, you'll get to know functional programming. You'll learn how to design programs around message passing and recursion, creating process-oriented programs focused more on data flow.

You'll also be better prepared to read other books and conversations about Erlang.

How This Book Works

This book tries to tell a story with Erlang. You'll probably get the most out of it if you read it in order at least the first time, though you're always welcome to come back to find whatever bits and pieces you need.

You'll start by getting Erlang installed and running, and looking around its shell. You'll spend a lot of time in the shell, so get cozy. Next, you'll start loading code into the shell to make it easier to write programs, and you'll learn how to call that code and mix it up.

Next, you'll take a close look at numbers because they're an easy place to get familiar with Erlang's basic structures. Then you'll learn about atoms, pattern-matching, and guards—the likely foundations of your program structure. After that you'll learn about strings, lists, and the recursion at the heart of most Erlang processing. Once you've gone a few million recursions down and back, it'll be time to look at processes, a key part of Erlang that relies on the message-passing model to support concurrency and resilience.

Once you have the foundation set, you can take a closer look at debugging and data storage, and then get a quick look at a toolset that is likely at the heart of your long-term development with Erlang: the Open Telecom Platform (OTP), which is about much much more than telephones.

Some people want to learn programming languages through a dictionary—here's a list of operators, here's a list of control structures, these are the datatypes—and then smash them together. Those lists are here, but they're in Appendix A, not in the main flow of the book.

Many of the examples I use are built on the same foundation. While you will probably be tired of falling objects by the end of the book, staying with a small set of examples makes it easier to introduce new features rather than explaining endless projects.

The main point you should get from this book is that you can program in Erlang. If you don't get that, let me know!

Etudes for Erlang

While I was writing this book, J. David Eisenberg was developing a broad set of exercises to accompany it. They proved comprehensive enough to become a separate project, which you can find (for free on the web) on GitHub (*https://github.com/oreil lymedia/etudes-for-erlang*). The front page is about contributing to the project, but if you click on a chapter name you'll get to the content.

The etudes are structured to match this book, but have grown over time to cover a slightly larger scope than this book does. You'll probably get the most out of them if you explore them each time you finish a chapter, but they're also great for general review and to test your understanding.

Why I Wrote This Book

I'm not an Erlang expert hoping to create more Erlang experts to get a lot of work done.

I'm a writer and developer who encountered Erlang, thought it was the programming language I'd been seeking for a long time, and felt compelled to share some of that. I'm hoping that the path I followed will work for other people, probably with variations, and that a book written from a beginner's perspective (and vetted by experts) will help more people find and enjoy Erlang.

Other Resources

This book may not be the best way for you to learn Erlang. It all depends on what you want to learn and why.

If your primary interest in learning Erlang is to break out of a programming rut, you should explore Bruce Tate's wild tour of *Seven Languages in Seven Weeks* (Pragmatic Publishers), which explores Ruby, Io, Prolog, Scala, Erlang, Clojure, and Haskell. Erlang gets only (an excellent) 37 pages, but that might be what you want.

For an online experience (now also in print from No Starch Books) with more snark and funnier illustrations, you should explore Fred Hebert's *Learn You Some Erlang for Great Good!* (*http://learnyousomeerlang.com/*). While much longer than Tate's telling, it certainly moves faster and may feel more like an experienced programmer's guide to Erlang.

The two classic general books on Erlang are the similarly titled *Programming Erlang* (Pragmatic Publishers) by Erlang creator Joe Armstrong, and *Erlang Programming* (O'Reilly) by Francesco Cesarini and Simon Thompson. They cover a lot of similar and overlapping terrain, and both may be good places to start if this book moves too slowly or you need more reference material. *Erlang Programming* goes further into what you can do with Erlang, whereas *Programming Erlang* provides a lot of detail on setting up an Erlang programming environment.

On the more advanced side, *Erlang and OTP in Action* (Manning) by Martin Logan, Eric Merritt, and Richard Carlsson, opens with a high-speed 72-page introduction to Erlang and then spends most of its time applying the OTP, Erlang's framework for building upgradeable and maintainable concurrent applications. More recently, *Designing for Scalability with Erlang/OTP* (O'Reilly), by Francesco Cesarini and Steve Vinoski, focuses squarely on building large and resilient applications with Erlang's OTP libraries.

At the end of each chapter of this book, you'll find a note pointing to relevant information on the chapter's content in other Erlang-focused books. Hopefully these notes will help you move quickly among them if you use this book as a companion to the rest of the growing Erlang library.

If you want to focus on connecting Erlang to the web, you should definitely also explore *Building Erlang Web Applications* (O'Reilly) by Zachary Kessin.

You'll also want to visit the main Erlang website (*http://www.erlang.org/*) for updates, downloads, documentation, and more.

Are You Sure You Want Erlang?

Though they've been obscure for a long time, there's a crowd of functional languages rising into greater popularity.

Six of them in particular—Elixir, Clojure, Scala, F#, Haskell, and OCaml—may be more appealing than Erlang if you have specific needs.

- Elixir is built on the same foundations as Erlang, but has a Ruby-like syntax with strong support for metaprogramming.
- Clojure and Scala run on the Java Virtual Machine (JVM), making them insanely portable, and they have access to Java libraries as a result. ClojureScript does the same with JavaScript, too. (Erjang makes it possible to run Erlang on the JVM, but it's not a core part of the language.)
- F# runs on the .NET Common Language Runtime (CLR), making it very portable in the Microsoft ecosystem, and again, has access to .NET libraries.
- Haskell, with deliberately mathematical roots, offers a stronger type system and a different kind of discipline (and laziness).
- OCaml also offers a strong type system, and focuses on performance.

Personally, I got my start with these concepts in XSLT. It's a very different kind of language meant for a specific domain of document transformation, but many of the same ideas flow through it.

You don't, of course, have to decide if Erlang is your life's dream now. You can learn concepts in Erlang and apply them elsewhere if another language turns out to be a better idea for your work.

Erlang Will Change You

Before you go deeper, you should know that working in Erlang may irrevocably change the way you look at programs. Its combination of functional code, process-orientation, and distributed development may seem alien at first. However, once it sinks in, Erlang can transform the way you solve problems, and potentially make it difficult to return to other languages, environments, and programming cultures.

Conventions Used in This Book

The following typographical conventions are used in this book:

Italic
> Indicates new terms, URLs, email addresses, filenames, and file extensions.

`Constant width`
> Used for program listings, as well as within paragraphs to refer to program elements such as variable or function names, statements, and keywords.

`Constant width bold`
> Shows commands or other text that should be typed literally by the user.

`Constant width italic`
> Shows text that should be replaced with user-supplied values or by values determined by context.

> This icon signifies a tip, suggestion, or general note.

> This icon indicates a warning or caution.

A Note on Erlang Syntax

Erlang's syntax seems to be a sticking point for a lot of people. It doesn't look like the C family of languages. Punctuation is different and capitalization matters. Periods even get used as conclusions rather than connectors!

To me, Erlang syntax mostly feels natural, and I'm especially happy that it's different from the other languages I typically use. I make a lot fewer mixups that way.

Rather than dwell on syntax, I've chosen just to present it as it is. Comparing it to other languages doesn't seem likely to be helpful, especially when different readers may come from different programming backgrounds. Hopefully you will find Erlang syntax as pleasant as I do. If you just can't get past it, you may want to try Elixir instead.

Using Code Examples

The examples in this book are meant to teach basic concepts in small bites. While you may certainly borrow code and reuse it as you see fit, you won't be able to take the code of this book and build a stupendous application instantly (unless perhaps you have an unusual fondness for calculating the speeds of falling objects).

The examples in this book are deliberately simple and perhaps even stupid. They aren't designed to dazzle or to show off, but to let you figure out how pieces fit together in the simplest possible way. You should, however, be able to figure out the steps you need to take to build a great application.

You can download the code from the Examples link on GitHub (*https://github.com/simonstl/introducing-erlang-2nd/*).

This book is here to help you get your job done. In general, you may use the code in this book in your programs and documentation. You do not need to contact us for permission unless you are reproducing a significant portion of the code. For example, writing a program that uses several chunks of code from this book does not require permission. Selling or distributing a CD-ROM of examples from O'Reilly books does require permission. Answering a question by citing this book and quoting example code does not require permission. Incorporating a significant amount of example code from this book into your product's documentation does require permission.

We appreciate, but do not require, attribution. An attribution usually includes the title, author, publisher, and ISBN. For example: "*Introducing Erlang*, 2nd Edition, by Simon St.Laurent (O'Reilly). Copyright 2017 Simon St.Laurent, 978-1-4919-7337-0."

If you feel your use of code examples falls outside fair use or the permission given above, feel free to contact us at *permissions@oreilly.com*.

Help This Book Grow

While I hope that you will enjoy reading this book and learn from it, I also hope that you can contribute to helping other readers learn Erlang here. You can help your fellow readers in a number of ways:

- If you find specific technical problems, bad explanations, or things that can be improved, please report them through the errata system.
- If you like (or don't like) the book, please leave reviews. The most visible places to do so are on Amazon.com (or its international sites) and at the O'Reilly catalog page (*http://bit.ly/introducing-erlang-2e*). Detailed explanations of what worked

and what didn't work for you (and the broader target audience of programmers new to Erlang) are helpful to other readers and to me.

- If you find you have much more you want to say about Erlang, please consider sharing it, whether on the web, in a book of your own, in training classes, or in whatever form you find easiest.

I'll update the book for errata, and try to address issues raised in reviews. Even once the book is "complete," I may still add some extra pieces to it. If you purchased it as an ebook, you'll receive these updates for free at least up to the point where it's time for a whole new edition. I don't expect that new edition declaration to come quickly, however, unless the Erlang world changes substantially.

Hopefully this book will engage you enough to make you consider sharing.

Please Use It For Good

I'll let you determine what "good" means, but think about it. Please try to use Erlang's power for projects that make the world a better place, or at least not a worse place.

O'Reilly Safari

 *Safari* (formerly Safari Books Online) is a membership-based training and reference platform for enterprise, government, educators, and individuals.

Members have access to thousands of books, training videos, Learning Paths, interactive tutorials, and curated playlists from over 250 publishers, including O'Reilly Media, Harvard Business Review, Prentice Hall Professional, Addison-Wesley Professional, Microsoft Press, Sams, Que, Peachpit Press, Adobe, Focal Press, Cisco Press, John Wiley & Sons, Syngress, Morgan Kaufmann, IBM Redbooks, Packt, Adobe Press, FT Press, Apress, Manning, New Riders, McGraw-Hill, Jones & Bartlett, and Course Technology, among others.

For more information, please visit *http://oreilly.com/safari*.

How to Contact Us

Please address comments and questions concerning this book to the publisher:

O'Reilly Media, Inc.
1005 Gravenstein Highway North
Sebastopol, CA 95472
800-998-9938 (in the United States or Canada)

707-829-0515 (international or local)

707-829-0104 (fax)

We have a web page for this book, where we list errata, examples, and any additional information. You can access this page at *http://bit.ly/introducing-erlang-2e*.

To comment or ask technical questions about this book, send email to *bookquestions@oreilly.com*.

For more information about our books, courses, conferences, and news, see our website at *http://www.oreilly.com*.

Find us on Facebook: *http://facebook.com/oreilly*

Follow us on Twitter: *http://twitter.com/oreillymedia*

Watch us on YouTube: *http://www.youtube.com/oreillymedia*

Acknowledgments

Many thanks to Zachary Kessin for introducing me to Erlang in the first place, and to him and Francesco Cesarini for encouraging me to write this. Detailed feedback from Steve Vinoski and Fred Hebert made it possible, I hope, for the first edition of this book, to get readers started on the right track. J. David Eisenberg and Chuck Ha helped make it especially possible for beginners to get started right, pointing out gaps and issues in my prose. Steve Vinoski's continued technical assistance on the second edition has improved the book further, and Dawn Schanafelt's editorial assistance on the second edition has made the prose much smoother.

In particular, thanks to my wife, Angelika, for encouraging me to finish this, to my son Konrad for not throwing the printouts around too much, and to my daughter Sungiva for understanding that after I told her the story about Ned and Ernie, adventuring snakes, I needed to go back downstairs and work on this.

CHAPTER 1

Getting Comfortable

Erlang has a tricky learning curve for many people. It starts gently for a little while, then gets much much steeper as you realize the discipline involved, and then goes nearly vertical for a little while as you try to figure out how that discipline affects getting work done—and then it's suddenly calm and peaceful with a gentle grade for a long time as you reapply what you've learned in different contexts.

Before that climb, it's best to get comfortable in the sunny meadows at the bottom of the learning curve. Erlang's shell, its command-line interface, is a cozy place to get started and a good place to start figuring out what works and what doesn't work in Erlang. Its features will spare you headaches later, so settle in!

Installation

Erlang is officially available from *http://www.erlang.org/download.html*. For this edition, I used Erlang/OTP 19, but any version of Erlang more recent than 17 should work. (Ericsson reliably releases a new version of Erlang every year or so.)

If you're on Windows, it's easy. Download the Windows binary file, run the installer, and you're set. If you are a brave beginner tackling your first programming language, this approach is easily your best bet.

On Linux or macOS, you may be able to download the source file and compile it. If the compilation approach doesn't work or isn't for you, Erlang Solutions offers a number of installs at *https://www.erlang-solutions.com/resources/download.html*. Also, many different package managers (Debian, Ubuntu, MacPorts, Brew, and so on) include Erlang. It may not be the very latest version, but having Erlang running is much better than not having Erlang running.

Erlang is increasingly part of the default installation on many systems, including Ubuntu Linux, largely thanks to the spread of CouchDB.

Firing It Up

On Mac OS X or Linux, go to the command line and type **erl**. On Windows, go to the command line and type **werl**.

You'll see something like the following code sample, likely with a cursor next to the 1> prompt:

```
lang/OTP 19 [erts-8.2] [64-bit] [smp:8:8] [async-threads:10]

Eshell V8.2  (abort with ^G)

1>
```

You're in Erlang!

First Steps: The Shell

Before moving on to the excitement of programming Erlang, it's worth noting how to quit. The shell suggests ^G, Ctrl-G, which will bring you to a mysterious (for now) user switch command. (Ctrl-C will bring you to a menu.) The simplest way to quit, allowing everything that might be running in the shell to exit normally, is q().:

```
1> q().
ok
2> SimonMacBook:~ simonstl$
```

So what have you done here? You've issued a shell command, calling a function q that itself calls the init:stop() function built into Erlang. The period after the command tells Erlang you're done with the line. It reports back with ok, prints a new line number (it always does that after a period), and drops you back out to the regular command line, in this case a bash shell on your laptop.

If you had left off the period after q(), the results would look a little different. You'd have started a new line but the command count wouldn't update, so the line would still start with 1>. When this happens, you can just type . and press Enter to finish your command:

```
1> q()
1> .
ok
2> SimonMacBook:~ simonstl$
```

Including the period at the end of the line will soon become second nature, but leaving it off can create a lot of confusion at the start.

 Quitting Erlang with q(). turns off everything Erlang is doing, period. That's fine when you're working locally, but will become a bad idea when you're connecting to a remote shell. To quit the shell without the risk of shutting down the Erlang runtime on another system, try Ctrl-G and then entering q, followed by the Enter key.

Moving through Text

If you explore the shell, you'll find that many things work the way they do in other shells. The left and right arrow keys move you backward and forward through the line you're editing. Some of the key bindings echo the emacs text editor. Ctrl-A will take you to the beginning of a line, while Ctrl-E will take you back to the end of the line. If you get two characters in the wrong sequence, pressing Ctrl-T will transpose them.

Like most Unix shells, pressing the Tab key will make the shell try to autocomplete what you've written, though in this case it's looking for module or function names (you'll see them soon), not filenames.

Also, as you type closing parentheses or square brackets, the cursor will highlight the corresponding opening parenthesis or square bracket.

Moving through History

The up and down arrow keys run through the history, making it easy to reissue commands.

When you use the up and down arrows, the history will be broken down by newlines, not by periods, so if you left a period off in a prior command you'll need to add it again. If you want to see what's in the history, try h(). You can also specify how much history to keep around with history(N) and results(N). You can tell Erlang to execute a given line again with e(N), and reference a given result value with v(N). Those line numbers can be useful!

Moving through Files

The Erlang shell does understand filesystems to some extent because you may need to move through them to reach the files that will become part of your program. The commands have the same names as Unix commands but are expressed as functions.

The Erlang shell starts wherever you opened the shell, and you can figure out where that is with pwd():

```
4> pwd().
/Users/simonstl
ok
5>
```

To change directories, use the cd() command, but you'll need to wrap the argument not only in parentheses but also in quotes, preferably double quotes:

```
5> cd(..).
* 1: syntax error before: '..'
5> cd("..").
/Users
ok
6> cd("simonstl").
/Users/simonstl
ok
7>
```

You can look around with the ls() command, which will list files in the current directory if you give it no arguments, and list files in a specified directory if you give it one argument.

Doing Something

One of the easiest ways to get started playing with Erlang is to use the shell as a calculator. You can enter mathematical expressions and get useful results:

```
Eshell V5.9  (abort with ^G)
1> 2+2.
4
2> 27-14.
13
3> 35*42023943.
1470838005
4> 200/15.
13.333333333333334
5> 200 div 15.
13
6> 200 rem 15.
5
7> 3*(4+15).
57
```

The first three operators are addition (+), subtraction (-), and multiplication (*), which work the same way whether you're working with integer values or floating points. The fourth, /, supports division where you expect a floating point (a number with a decimal part) result. If you want an integer result (and have integer arguments), use the `div` operator instead, with `rem` to get the remainder, as shown on lines 5 and 6. Parentheses let you modify the order in which operators are processed, as shown on line 7. (The normal order of operations is listed in Appendix A.)

Erlang will accept integers in place of floats, but floats are not always welcome where integers are used. If you need to convert a floating-point number to an integer, you can use the `round()` built-in function:

```
8> round(200/15).
13
```

The `round()` function drops the decimal part of the number. If the decimal part is greater than or equal to .5, it increases the integer part by 1, rounding up. If you'd rather just drop the decimal part completely, use the `trunc()` function, which effectively always rounds down.

You can also refer to a previous result by its line number using `v()`. For example:

```
9> 4*v(8).
52
```

The result on line 8 was 13, and 4*13 is 52.

If you're feeling adventurous, you can use negative numbers to reference prior results. `v(-1)` is the previous result, `v(-2)` is the result before that, and so on.

Calling Functions

If you want to do more powerful calculations, Erlang's `math` module offers pretty much the classic set of functions supported by a scientific calculator. The functions return floating-point values. The constant pi is available as a function, `math:pi()`. Trigonometric, logarithmic, exponential, square root, and (except on Windows) even the Gauss error functions are readily available. (The trigonometric functions take their arguments in radians, not degrees, so be ready to convert if necessary.) Using these functions is a little verbose because of the need to prefix them with `math:`, but it's still reasonably sane.

For example, to get the sine of zero radians, you'd write:

```
1> math:sin(0).
0.0
```

Note that it's `0.0`, not just `0`, indicating that the number is a floating point.

To calculate the cosine of pi and 2pi radians, you'd write:

```
2> math:cos(math:pi()).
-1.0
3> math:cos(2*math:pi()).
1.0
```

To calculate 2 taken to the 16th power, you'd use:

```
4> math:pow(2,16).
65536.0
```

The full set of mathematical functions supported by Erlang's math module is listed in Appendix A.

Numbers in Erlang

Erlang recognizes two kinds of numbers: integers and floating-point numbers (often called floats). It's easy to think of integers as "whole numbers," with no decimal part, and floats as "decimal numbers," with a decimal point and some value (even if it's 0) to the right of the decimal. 1 is an integer, 1.0 is a floating-point number.

However, it's a little trickier than that. Erlang treats integers and floats very differently from each other. Erlang lets you store massive numbers as integers, but whether they're big or small, they are always precise. You don't need to worry about their values being off by just a little.

Floats, on the other hand, cover a wide range of numbers but with limited precision. Erlang uses the 64-bit IEEE 754-1985 "double-precision" representation. This means that it keeps track of about 15 decimal digits plus an exponent. It can also represent some large numbers—powers up to positive or negative 308 are available—but because it tracks only a limited number of digits, results will vary a little more than may seem convenient, especially when you want to do comparisons:

```
1> 3487598347598347598437583475893475843749245.0.
3.4875983475983474e42
2> 2343243.34543589385023454333954 5.
2343243.3454358936
3> 0.0000000000000000000000000000002343243243243223423232 4.
2.3432432432432235e-30
```

As you can see, some digits get left behind, and the overall magnitude of the number is represented with an exponent.

When you enter floating-point numbers, you must always also have at least one number to the left of the decimal point, even if it's zero. Otherwise Erlang reports a syntax error—it doesn't understand what you're doing:

```
4> .0000000000000000000000000000002343243243243223423232 4.
* 1: syntax error before: 23432432432432234232324
```

You can also write floats using the digits plus exponent notation:

```
7> 2.923e127.
2.923e127
8> 7.6345435e-231.
7.6345435e-231
```

Floats' lack of precision can cause anomalous results. For example, the sine of zero is zero, and the sine of pi is also zero. However, if you calculate this in Erlang, you won't quite get to zero with the float approximation Erlang provides for pi:

```
1> math:sin(0).
0.0
2> math:sin(math:pi()).
1.2246467991473532e-16
```

If Erlang's representation of pi went further, and its calculations went further, the result for line 2 would be closer to zero.

If you need to keep track of money, integers are going to be a better bet. Use the smallest available unit—cents for US dollars, for instance—and remember that those cents are 1/100 of a dollar. (Financial transactions can go to much smaller fractions, but you'll still want to represent them as integers with a known multiplier.) For more complex calculations, though, you'll want to use floats, and just be aware that the results will be imprecise.

If you need to do calculations on integers using a base other than 10, you can use *Base#Value* notation. For example, if you wanted to specify the binary value of 1010111, you could write:

```
3> 2#1010111.
87
```

Erlang reports back with the base 10 value of the number. Similarly, you can specify hexadecimal numbers by using 16 instead of 2:

```
4> 16#cafe.
51966
```

Erlang lets you use either upper- or lowercase for hexdecimal numbers: 16#CAFE and 16#CaFe also produce 51966. You aren't limited to the traditional binary (base 2), octal (base 8), and hexadecimal (base 16) choices. If you want to work in base 18, or any base up to 36, you can:

```
5> 18#gaffe.
1743080
```

 Why might you use base 36? It's an extremely easy way to create keys that look like a combination of letters and numbers, but resolve neatly to numbers. The 6-digit codes airlines use to identify tickets, like G6ZV1N, are easily treated as base 36. (However, they usually leave out some digits and letters that are easily confused, such as 0 and O, and 1 and l.)

To make any of these numbers negative just put a minus sign (-) in front of them. This works with normal integers, *Base#Value* notation, and floats:

```
6> -1234.
-1234
7> -16#cafe.
-51966
8> -2.045234324e6.
-2045234.324
```

Working with Variables in the Shell

The v() function lets you refer to the results of previous expressions, but it's not exactly convenient to keep track of result numbers, and the v() function works only in the shell. It isn't a general-purpose mechanism. A more reasonable solution stores values with textual names, creating variables.

Erlang variable names begin with a capital letter or an underscore. Normal variables start with a capital letter, whereas underscores start "don't care" variables, variables you don't actually intend to use. For now, stick with normal variables. You assign a value to a variable using a syntax that should be familiar from algebra or other programming languages, here N is used as the variable:

```
1> N=1.
1
```

To see the value of a variable, just type its name:

```
2> N.
1
```

To see Erlang protest at your rude behavior, try assigning the variable a new value:

```
3> N=2.
** exception error: no match of right-hand side value 2
4> N=N+1.
** exception error: no match of right-hand side value 2
```

What's happening here? Erlang expects the right-hand side of an expression, after the =, to match the left-hand side. It's willing to make that happen if a variable on the left side isn't bound yet, as was the case with N=1 in the first line. However, once the variable N is set to 1, Erlang interprets N=2 as 1=2, which it won't accept. N=N+1 also evaluates to 1=2, and doesn't work. Erlang's *single assignment* model, where each variable can be assigned a value only once in a given context, imposes discipline whose value you will see in later chapters.

Erlang expressions work like algebra, where N never equals N+1. It just can't happen that way. However, once you've set N to 1, it's fine to try expressions that also come to one:

```
5> N=2-1.
1
6> N=15 div (3*5).
1
```

This will get much more important when you start to take advantage of Erlang's pattern-matching capabilities. You can also write the following:

```
7> 1=N.
1
```

Erlang won't attempt to bind any variables when they appear on the right side of the equals sign, and this just effectively asks Erlang to compare 1 to 1. Try it with 2, however, and Erlang complains that there isn't a match; 2 does not equal 1:

```
8> 2=N.
** exception error: no match of right-hand side value 1
```

You can also use bound variables in calculations, for example to create new bound variables. Here's one called Number:

```
9> Number=N*4+N.
5
10> 6*Number.
30
```

When you assign a value to a variable, you should make sure that all the calculations are on the right side of the equals sign. Even though I know that M should be 6 when 2*M = 3*4, Erlang doesn't:

```
11> 2*M=3*4.
* 1: illegal pattern
```

The shell will remember your variables until you quit or tell it to forget them. Code in Erlang functions doesn't forget, until the functions stop running.

Seeing Your Bound Variables

After poking around the shell for a while using it as a calculator (try it!), you may find you've forgotten what variables you've already bound. If you need a reminder, the b() shell command can help:

```
11> b().
N = 1
Number = 5
ok
```

Clearing Bound Variables in the Shell

In the shell, and only in the shell, you can clear all variable bindings or you can clear specific variable bindings. This may prove useful after an egregious typo or to reset your console for new calculations, but it isn't an option you'll have in regular code.

To clear a specific variable, removing its binding and letting you set a new value, use the f() function, giving the variable name as an argument:

```
12> f(N).
ok
13> b().
Number = 5
ok
14> N=2.
2
```

To clear all the bound variables in the shell, just call f() with no arguments:

```
15> b().
N = 2
Number = 5
ok
16> f().
ok
17> b().
ok
```

They all disappeared.

Before moving on to the next chapter, which will introduce modules and functions, spend some time playing in the Erlang shell. The experience, even at this simple level, will help you move forward. Use variables, and see what happens with large integers. Erlang supports large numbers very well. Try mixing numbers with decimal values (floats) and integers in calculations, and see what happens. Nothing should be difficult yet, though I suspect the idea of variables that don't change values gives you a hint of what's to come.

You can learn more about installation and working with the shell in Chapter 2 of *Erlang Programming* (O'Reilly); Chapters 2 and 3 of *Programming Erlang* 2nd Edition (Pragmatic); Section 2.1 of *Erlang and OTP in Action* (Manning); and Chapter 1 of *Learn You Some Erlang For Great Good!* (No Starch Press).

Functions and Modules

Like most programming languages, Erlang lets you define functions to help you represent repeated calculations. While Erlang functions can become complicated, they start out reasonably simple.

Fun with fun

Erlang provides a tool for creating functions in the shell, the appropriately named fun. For example, to create a function that calculates the velocity of a falling object based on the distance it drops in meters, you could create the following:

```
1> FallVelocity = fun(Distance) -> math:sqrt(2 * 9.8 * Distance) end.
#Fun<erl_eval.6.111823515>
```

You can read that as a pattern match that binds the variable FallVelocity to a function that takes an argument of Distance. The function returns (I like to read the -> as "yields") the square root of 2 times a gravitational constant for Earth of 9.8 m/s squared, times Distance (in meters). Then the function comes to an end, and a period closes the statement.

 If you want to include multiple statements in a function defined by a fun, separate them with commas, like FallVelocity = fun(Distance) -> X = (2 * 9.8 * Distance), math:sqrt(X) end. You can read the commas as *and*.

The return value in the shell, #Fun<erl_eval.6.111823515>, isn't especially meaningful by itself, but it tells you that you've created a function and didn't just get an error. The number in the return value will probably be different. If you want a slightly more detailed sign that Erlang understood you, you can use the b() shell command to see what it thinks:

```
2> b().
FallVelocity =
    fun(Distance) ->
            math:sqrt(2 * 9.8 * Distance)
    end
ok
```

Conveniently, binding the function to the variable FallVelocity lets you use that variable to calculate the velocity of objects falling to Earth:

```
3> FallVelocity(20).
19.79898987322333
4> FallVelocity(200).
62.609903369994115
5> FallVelocity(2000).
197.9898987322333
```

If you want those meters per second in miles per hour, just create another function. You can copy and paste the earlier results into it (as I did here), or pick shorter numbers:

```
6> Mps_to_mph = fun(Mps) -> 2.23693629 * Mps end.
#Fun<erl_eval.6.111823515>
7> Mps_to_mph(19.79898987322333).
44.289078952755766
8> Mps_to_mph(62.609903369994115).
140.05436496173314
9> Mps_to_mph(197.9898987322333).
442.89078952755773
```

I think I'll stay away from 2000-meter drops. Prefer the fall speed in kilometers per hour?

```
10> Mps_to_kph = fun(Mps) -> 3.6 * Mps end.
#Fun<erl_eval.6.111823515>
11> Mps_to_kph(19.79898987322333).
71.27636354360399
12> Mps_to_kph(62.609903369994115).
225.3956521319788
13> Mps_to_kph(197.9898987322333).
712.76363543604
```

You can also go straight to your preferred measurement by nesting the following calls:

```
14> Mps_to_kph(FallVelocity(2000)).
712.76363543604
```

However you represent it, that's really fast, though air resistance will slow those down a lot in reality.

This is handy for repeated calculations, but you probably don't want to push this kind of function use too far in the shell, as flushing your variables or quitting the shell session makes your functions vanish.

 If you get an error that looks like `** exception error: no function clause matching erl_eval:'-inside-an-interpreted-fun-'` (value), check your capitalization. It may take a while to get used to capitalizing all your variables, including arguments in functions.

Defining Modules

Most Erlang programs define their functions in compiled modules rather than in the shell. Modules are a more formal place to put programs, and they give you the ability to store, encapsulate, share, and manage your code more effectively.

Each module should go in its own file, with an extension of *.erl*. You should use *name_of_module.erl*, where *name_of_module* is the name you specify inside of the module file. Example 2-1, which you can find in the examples archive at *ch02/ex1-drop*, shows what a module, *drop.erl*, containing the functions previously defined might look like.

Example 2-1. Module for calculating and converting fall velocities

```
-module(drop).
-export([fall_velocity/1, mps_to_mph/1, mps_to_kph/1]).

fall_velocity(Distance) -> math:sqrt(2 * 9.8 * Distance).

mps_to_mph(Mps) -> 2.23693629 * Mps.

mps_to_kph(Mps) -> 3.6 * Mps.
```

There are two key kinds of information in this module. At the top, the `-module` and the `-export` directives tell the compiler key things about the module—its name and which functions it should make visible to other code that uses this module. The `-export` directive gives a list of functions that should be made visible—not just their names, but their *arity*, the number of arguments they take. Erlang considers functions with the same name but different arity to be different functions.

All of the code in a module must be contained in functions.

Below the directives is a set of expressions defining functions, which look similar to the `fun` declarations used earlier but not quite the same. The function names start with lowercase, not uppercase, and the syntax is slightly different. `fun` and `end` don't appear, and the function name is immediately followed by parentheses containing a set of arguments.

 If you get errors like "drop.erl:2: bad function arity drop.erl:6: syntax error before: Fall_velocity", it's probably because you didn't convert the names from your fun/s so they start with a lowercase letter.

How do you make this module actually do something?

It's time to start compiling Erlang code. The shell will let you compile modules and then use them immediately. The c() function lets you compile code. You don't need to (and shouldn't) include the .erl file extension in the name you pass to c(), though you can specify directory paths.

```
1> ls().
drop.erl
ok
2> c(drop).
{ok,drop}
3> ls().
drop.beam      drop.erl
ok
```

Line 1 checks to see if the *drop.erl* source file is there, and shows the directory listing. Line 2 actually compiles it, and line 3 shows that a new file, *drop.beam*, is now available.

 While you can compile code in another directory by specifying the directory path, the compiled code will end up in your current working directory. I prefer to be in the same directory as the file, whether I started the Erlang shell from there or navigated there with the commands shown in the previous chapter. For small projects, that tends to keep things more findable.

Now that you have *drop.beam*, you can call functions from the module. You need to prefix those calls with drop, as shown in lines 4 and 5 of the following code.

```
4> drop:fall_velocity(20).
19.79898987322333
5> drop:mps_to_mph(drop:fall_velocity(20)).
44.289078952755766
```

It works the same as its predecessors, but now you can quit the shell, return, and still use the compiled functions.

```
6> q().
ok
$ erl
Erlang/OTP 19 [erts-8.2] [64-bit] [smp:8:8] [async-threads:10]

Eshell V8.2  (abort with ^G)

1> drop:mps_to_mph(drop:fall_velocity(20)).
44.289078952755766
```

Most Erlang programming (beyond tinkering in the shell) is creating functions in modules and connecting them into larger programs.

Erlang Compilation and the Runtime System

When you write Erlang in the shell, it has to interpret every command, even if you've written it before. When you tell Erlang to compile a file, it converts your text into something it can process without having to reinterpret all the text, tremendously improving efficiency when you run the code.

That "something it can process," in Erlang's case, is a BEAM file. It contains code that the BEAM processor, a key piece of the Erlang runtime system (ERTS), can run. BEAM is Bogdan's Erlang Abstract Machine, a virtual machine that interprets optimized BEAM code. This may sound slightly less efficient than the traditional compilation to machine code that runs directly on the computer, but it resembles other virtual machines. (Oracle's Java Virtual Machine (JVM) and the Common Language Runtime used by Microsoft's .NET Framework are the two most common virtual machines.)

Having its own virtual machine and runtime system lets Erlang optimize some key things, making it easier to build applications that scale reliably. Its process scheduler simplifies distributing work across multiple processors in a single computer. You don't have to think about how many processors your application might get to use—you just write independent processes, and Erlang spreads them out. Erlang also manages input and output in its own way, avoiding connection styles that block other processing. The virtual machine also uses a garbage-collection strategy that fits its style of processing, allowing for briefer pauses in program execution. (Garbage collection releases memory that processes needed at one point but are no longer using.)

When you create and deliver Erlang programs, you will be distributing them as a set of compiled BEAM files. But you don't need to compile each one from the shell as we're doing here. erlc will let you compile Erlang files directly and combine that compilation into make tasks and similar things, whereas escript can compile or interpret and run Erlang code from outside of the Erlang shell.

From Module to fun

If you like the style of code that fun allowed but also want your code stored more reliably in modules where it's easier to debug, you can get the best of both worlds by using the fun keyword to refer to a function you've already defined. To do that, you *don't* use parentheses after fun, and give the module name, function name, and arity.

```
1> F_v = fun drop:fall_velocity/1.
#Fun<drop.fall_velocity.1>
2> F_v(20).
19.79898987322333
```

You can also do this within code in a module, and if you're referring to code in the same module, you can leave off the module name preface. (In this case, that would mean leaving off drop: and just using fall_velocity/1.)

Functions and Variable Scope

Erlang lets you bind a variable only once, but you might call a function many times over the course of a program. Doesn't that mean the same variable will be bound many times?

Yes, it will be bound many times but always in separate contexts. Erlang doesn't consider multiple calls to the same function to be the same thing. It starts with a fresh set of unassigned variables every time you call that function.

Similarly, Erlang doesn't worry if you use the same variable name in different functions or function clauses. They aren't going to be called in the same context at the same time, so there isn't a collision.

The place you need to avoid reassigning values to an already bound variable is within a given path through a given function. As long as you don't try to reuse a variable in a given context, you shouldn't have to worry.

Module Directives

By default, modules have very thick walls, and everything inside of them is considered private. Everything going in or out of the module needs a pass to do so, and you grant those passes through module directives (sometimes called module attributes).

The preceding example showed two module directives—-module and -export. The -module directive sets the name for the module, which outside code will need to know in order to call the functions. The -export directive specifies the functions that outside code can reach.

This version of the drop module mixes two different kinds of functions. The fall_velocity/1 function fits the name of the module, drop, very well, providing a calculation based on the height from which an object falls. The `mps_to_mph/1` and `mps_to_kph/1` functions, however, aren't about dropping. They are generic measurement-conversion functions that are useful in other contexts and really belong in their own module. Examples 2-2 and 2-3, both in *ch02/ex2-combined*, show how this might be improved.

Example 2-2. Module for calculating fall velocities

```
-module(drop).
-export([fall_velocity/1]).

fall_velocity(Distance) -> math:sqrt(2 * 9.8 * Distance).
```

Example 2-3. Module for converting fall velocities

```
-module(convert).
-export([mps_to_mph/1, mps_to_kph/1]).

mps_to_mph(Mps) -> 2.23693629 * Mps.

mps_to_kph(Mps) -> 3.6 * Mps.
```

Next, you can compile them, and then the separated functions are available for use:

```
Eshell V5.9  (abort with ^G)
1> c(drop).
{ok,drop}
2> c(convert).
{ok,convert}
3> ls().
convert.beam    convert.erl    drop.beam    drop.erl

ok
4> convert:mps_to_mph(drop:fall_velocity(20)).
44.289078952755766
```

That reads more neatly, but how might this code work if a third module needed to call those functions? Modules that call code from other modules need to specify that explicitly. Example 2-4, in *ch02/ex3-combined*, shows a module that uses functions from both the drop and convert modules.

Example 2-4. Module for combining drop and convert logic

```
-module(combined).
-export([height_to_mph/1]).

height_to_mph(Meters) -> convert:mps_to_mph(drop:fall_velocity(Meters)).
```

That looks much like the way you called it from the Erlang shell, but if you have a lot of calls to external modules, that can get verbose quickly. The -import directive, shown in Example 2-5, lets you simplify your code, though it comes with the risk of confusing other people who think the imported functions must be defined within this module. (You can find this in *ch02/ex4-combined*.)

Example 2-5. Module for combining drop and convert logic using import

```
-module(combined).
-export([height_to_mph/1]).
-import(drop, [fall_velocity/1]).
-import(convert, [mps_to_mph/1]).

height_to_mph(Meters) -> mps_to_mph(fall_velocity(Meters)).
```

For now, it's probably best to know about the -import directive so you can read other people's code, but not to use it unless you just can't resist. It can make it harder to figure out where bugs are coming from, which may cost you more time than the extra typing.

Erlang includes one other directive that's similarly convenient but not best practice to use: -compile(export_all). That directive tears down the module wall, making all functions available for external calls. In a module where everything is supposed to be public, that might save you typing out all the functions and all the arities of your module. However, it also means anyone can call anything in your code, exposing a lot more surface area for misunderstandings and complex debugging. If you just can't resist, it's available, but try to resist.

 You can also make up your own user directives. -author(Name) and -date(Date) are commonly used. If you make up your own directives, they can have only one argument. If you spend enough time in Erlang, you'll also encounter the following directives: -behaviour(Behaviour), -record(Name, Fields), and -vsn(Version).

Documenting Code

Your programs can run perfectly well without documentation. Your projects, however, will have a much harder time.

While programmers like to think they write code that anyone can look at and sort out, the painful reality is that code even a little more complicated than that shown in the previous examples can prove mystifying to other developers. If you step away from code for a while, the understanding you developed while programming it may have faded, and even your own code can seem incomprehensible.

The simplest way to add more explicit explanations to your code is to insert comments. You can start a comment with %, and it runs to the end of the line. Some comments take up an entire line, while others are short snippets at the end of a line. Example 2-6 shows both varieties of comments.

Example 2-6. Comments in action

```erlang
-module(combined).
-export([height_to_mph/1]).    % there will be more soon!

%%% combines logic from other modules into a convenience function.
height_to_mph(Meters) -> convert:mps_to_mph(drop:fall_velocity(Meters)).
```

The Erlang compiler will ignore all text between the % sign and the end of the line, but humans exploring the code will be able to read them.

Why are there multiple percent signs at the start of the line? The Erlang Emacs mode and many other Erlang tools expect the number of percent signs to indicate levels of indentation. Three percent signs (%%%) mean the comment will be formatted flush left, two percent signs (%%) mean the comment is indented with surrounding code, and a single percent sign (%) is used for comments on the end of a line.

Informal comments are useful, but developers have a habit of including comments that help them keep track of what they're doing while they're writing the code. Those comments may or may not be what other developers need to understand the code, or even what you need when you return to the code after a long time away. More formal comment structures may be more work than you want to take on in the heat of a programming session, but they also force you to think about who might be looking at your code in the future and what they might want to know.

Erlang includes a documentation system called *EDoc*, which converts comments placed in the code into navigable HTML documentation. It relies on specially formatted comments, a directive, and occasionally an extra file to provide structured information about your modules and application.

Documenting Modules

The modules in this chapter are very simple so far, but there is enough there to start documenting, as shown in the files at *ch02/ex5-docs*. Example 2-7 presents the drop module with more information about who created it and why.

Example 2-7. Documented module for calculating fall velocities

```erlang
%% @author Simon St.Laurent <simonstl@simonstl.com> [http://simonstl.com]
%% @doc Functions calculating velocities achieved by objects
%% dropped in a vacuum.
```

```
%% @reference from <a href= "http://shop.oreilly.com/product/0636920025818.do" >
%% Introducing Erlang</a>,
%% O'Reilly Media, Inc., 2017.
%% @copyright 2017 by Simon St.Laurent
%% @version 0.1

-module(drop).
-export([fall_velocity/1]).

fall_velocity(Distance) -> math:sqrt(2 * 9.8 * Distance).
```

Erlang can build the files for you using the EDoc `file` function:

```
Eshell V5.9  (abort with ^G)
1> edoc:files(["drop.erl"], [{dir, "doc"}]).
ok
```

You'll now have a collection of files in the *doc* subdirectory. If you open *drop.html* in a browser, you'll see something like Figure 2-1.

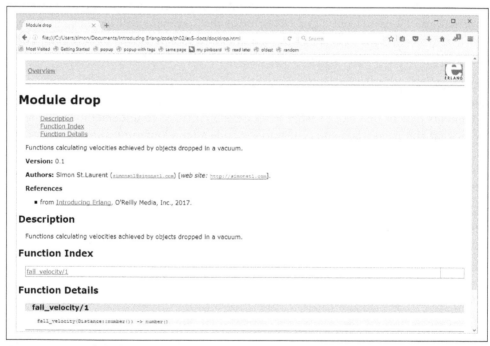

Figure 2-1. Module documentation generated from the drop.erl file

All of that metadata is great, and it can be gratifying to see your name "in lights." However, unless you have a complex story to tell about your module as a whole, it's likely that the core of the documentation will appear at the function level.

Documenting Functions

The drop module contains one function: fall_velocity/1. You probably know that it takes a distance in meters and returns a velocity in meters per second for an object dropped in a vacuum on Earth, but the code doesn't actually say that. Example 2-8 shows how to fix that with EDoc comments and the @doc tag.

Example 2-8. Documented function for calculating fall velocities

```
%% @doc Calculates the velocity of an object falling on Earth
%% as if it were in a vacuum (no air resistance).  The distance is
%% the height from which the object falls, specified in meters,
%% and the function returns a velocity in meters per second.

fall_velocity(Distance) -> math:sqrt(2 * 9.8 * Distance).
```

Figure 2-2 shows the result, which is considerably more helpful than the previous blank space around the function. It neatly takes the first sentence of the information following @doc and puts it in the index, using the whole description for the Function Details section. You can also use XHTML markup in the @doc section.

Figure 2-2. Function documentation generated from the drop.erl file

That's a major improvement, but what if a user specifies "twenty" meters instead of 20 meters? Because Erlang doesn't worry much about types, the Erlang code doesn't say that the value for `Distance` has to be a number or the function will return an error.

You can add a directive, `-spec`, to add that information. In some ways it feels like a duplicate of the method declaration. In this case, it's simple, as shown in Example 2-9.

Example 2-9. Documented function for calculating fall velocities

```
%% @doc Calculates the velocity of an object falling on Earth
%% as if it was in a vacuum (no air resistance).  The distance is
%% the height from which the object falls, specified in meters,
%% and the function returns a velocity in meters per second.

-spec(fall_velocity(number()) -> number()).

fall_velocity(Distance) -> math:sqrt(2 * 9.8 * Distance).
```

EDoc will combine the types specified in the `-spec` directive with the parameter names in the actual function declaration to produce the documentation shown in Figure 2-3.

Figure 2-3. EDoc documentation with type information

This chapter has really demonstrated only the number() type, which combines integer() and float(). Appendix A includes a full list of types. If you really want to explore types in Erlang, Dialyzer is the primary tool at the moment.

Documenting Your Application

Sometimes you want information like the author and copyright data to appear in every module, often when it varies from module to module. Other times that becomes clutter, and it's easier to put it into one place where it applies to all of your modules.

You can create an *overview.edoc* file in your project's *doc* directory. Its content looks much like the markup used in the modules, but because it isn't mixed with code, you don't need to preface every line with %%. The *overview.edoc* file for this project might look like Example 2-10.

Example 2-10. Documented module for calculating fall velocities

```
@author Simon St.Laurent <simonstl@simonstl.com> [http://simonstl.com]
@doc Functions for calculating and converting velocities.
@reference from <a href= "http://shop.oreilly.com/product/0636920056690.do"
>Introducing Erlang</a>, O'Reilly Media, Inc., 2017.
@copyright 2017 by Simon St.Laurent
@version 0.1
```

Now, if you regenerate documentation and click on the Overview link, you'll see something like Figure 2-4.

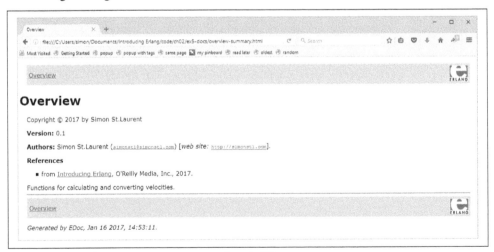

Figure 2-4. Application overview created with EDoc

If you create similar documentation in each of the Erlang files and run `edoc:files(["drop.erl", "convert.erl", "combined.erl"]).` in the Erlang shell, EDoc will build a neat if somewhat plain set of frame-based documentation for your application, as shown in Figure 2-5.

Figure 2-5. The opening to the complete set of module documentation

This is just an introduction to EDoc. For more, see Chapter 18 of *Erlang Programming*, where you can learn about fun things like the `@todo` tag.

You can learn more about working with functions and modules in Chapters 2, 3, and 9 of *Erlang Programming* (O'Reilly); Chapter 4 of *Programming Erlang*, 2nd Edition (Pragmatic); Sections 2.3, 2.5, and 2.7 of *Erlang and OTP in Action* (Manning); and Chapters 2 and 3 of *Learn You Some Erlang For Great Good!* (No Starch Press). There's more on documentation in Chapter 18 of *Erlang Programming* and types in Chapter 30 of *Learn You Some Erlang For Great Good!*.

CHAPTER 3

Atoms, Tuples, and Pattern Matching

Erlang programs are at heart a set of message requests and tools for processing them. Erlang provides tools that simplify the efficient handling of those messages, letting you create code that is readable (to programmers at least) while still running efficiently when you need speed.

Atoms

Atoms are key structures in Erlang. Technically they're just another type of data, but it's hard to overstate their impact on Erlang programming style.

Usually, atoms are bits of text that start with a lowercase letter, like ok or `earth`. They can also contain (though not start with) underscores (_) and at symbols (@), like `this_is_a_short_sentence` or `me@home`. If you want more freedom to start with uppercase letters or use spaces, you can put them in single quotes, like `'Today is a good day'`. Generally, the one-word lowercase form is easier to read.

Atoms have values, which are the same as their text. (Remember, the period after `hello` isn't part of the atom—it ends the expression.)

```
1> hello.
hello
```

That's not very exciting in itself. What makes atoms exciting is the way that they can combine with other types and Erlang's pattern-matching techniques to build simple but powerful logical structures.

Pattern Matching with Atoms

Erlang used pattern matching to make the examples in Chapter 2 work, but it was very simple. The name of the function was the one key piece that varied, and as long as you provided a numeric argument Erlang knew what you meant. Erlang's pattern matching offers much more sophisticated possibilities, however, allowing you to match on arguments as well as on function names.

For example, suppose you want to calculate the velocity of falling objects not just on Earth, where the gravitational constant is 9.8 meters per second squared, but on Earth's moon, where it is 1.6 meters per second squared, and on Mars, where it is 3.71 meters per second squared. Example 3-1, which you can find in *ch03/ex1-atoms*, shows one way to build code that supports this.

Example 3-1. Pattern matching on atoms as well as function names

```
-module(drop).
-export([fall_velocity/2]).


fall_velocity(earth, Distance) -> math:sqrt(2 * 9.8 * Distance);

fall_velocity(moon, Distance) -> math:sqrt(2 * 1.6 * Distance);

fall_velocity(mars, Distance) -> math:sqrt(2 * 3.71 * Distance).
```

It looks like the `fall_velocity` function gets defined three times here, and it certainly provides three processing paths for the same function. However, because those definitions are separated with semicolons, they are treated as choices—selected by pattern matching—rather than duplicate definitions. As in English grammar, these pieces are called *clauses*.

 If you use periods instead of semicolons, you'll get errors like `drop.erl:5: function fall_velocity/2 already defined`.

Once you have typed in this code, you can calculate velocities for objects falling a given distance on Earth, the Earth's moon, and Mars:

```
1> c(drop).
{ok,drop}
2> drop:fall_velocity(earth,20).
19.79898987322333
3> drop:fall_velocity(moon,20).
8.0
4> drop:fall_velocity(mars,20).
12.181953866272849
```

You'll quickly find that atoms are critical for writing readable Erlang code.

Atomic Booleans

Two of Erlang's atoms have special properties: `true` and `false`, representing the Boolean logic values of the same names. Erlang will return these atoms if you ask it to compare something:

```
1> 3<2.
false
2> 3>2.
true
3> 10 == 10.
true
```

Erlang also has special operators that work on these atoms (and on comparisons that resolve to these atoms):

```
1> true and true.
true
2> true and false.
false
3> true or false.
true
4> false or false.
false
5> true xor false.
true
6> true xor true.
false
7> not true.
false
```

The `and`, `or`, and `xor` operators take two arguments. For `and`, the result is true if and only if the two arguments are true. For `or`, the result is true if at least one of the arguments is true. For `xor`, exclusive or, the result is true if one but not both arguments is true. In all other cases, these three operators return false. If you're comparing expressions more complicated than `true` and `false`, it's wise to put them in parentheses.

 There are two additional operators for situations where you don't want or need to evaluate all of the arguments. The `andalso` operator behaves like `and` but evaluates the second argument only if the first one is true. The `orelse` operator evaluates the second argument only if the first one is false.

The `not` operator is simpler, taking just one argument. It turns `true` into `false` and `false` into `true`. Unlike the other Boolean operators, which go between their arguments, `not` goes before its single argument.

If you try to use these operators with any other atoms, you'll get a bad argument exception.

There are other atoms that have an accepted meaning, like ok and error, but those are more conventions than a formal part of the language.

Guards

The `fall_velocity` calculations work fairly well, but there's still one glitch: if the function gets a negative value for distance, the square root (`sqrt`) function in the calculation will be unhappy:

```
5> drop:fall_velocity(earth,-20).
** exception error: bad argument in an arithmetic expression
     in function  math:sqrt/1
         called as math:sqrt(-392.0)
     in call from drop:fall_velocity/2 (drop.erl, line 4)
```

Since you can't dig a hole 20 meters down, release an object, and marvel as it accelerates to the surface, this isn't a terrible result. However, it might be more elegant to at least produce a different kind of error.

In Erlang, you can specify which data a given function will accept with *guards*. Guards, indicated by the when keyword, let you fine-tune the pattern matching based on the content of arguments, not just their shape. Guards have to stay simple, can use only a very few built-in functions, and are limited by a requirement that they evaluate only data without any side effects, but they can still transform your code.

You can find a list of functions that can safely be used in guards in Appendix A.

Guards evaluate their expressions to `true` or `false`, as previously described, and the first one with a `true` result wins. That means you can write when true for a guard that always gets called if it is reached, or block out some code you don't want to call (for now) with when false.

In this simple case, you can keep negative numbers away from the square root function by adding guards to the `fall_velocity` clauses, as shown in Example 3-2, which you can find at *ch03/ex2-guards*.

Example 3-2. Adding guards to the function clauses

```
-module(drop).
-export([fall_velocity/2]).

fall_velocity(earth, Distance) when Distance >= 0  -> math:sqrt(2 * 9.8 * Distance);

fall_velocity(moon, Distance) when Distance >= 0 -> math:sqrt(2 * 1.6 * Distance);

fall_velocity(mars, Distance) when Distance >= 0 -> math:sqrt(2 * 3.71 * Distance).
```

 In Erlang, greater-than-or-equal-to is written as >=, and less-than-or-equal-to as =<. Don't make them look like arrows.

The when expression describes a condition or set of conditions in the function head. In this case, the condition is simple: the Distance must be greater than or equal to zero. If you compile that code and ask for the result of a negative distance, the result is different:

```
5> drop:fall_velocity(earth,-20).
** exception error: no function clause matching
    drop:fall_velocity(earth,-20) (drop.erl, line 12)
```

Because of the guard, Erlang doesn't find a function clause that works with a negative argument. The error message may not seem like a major improvement, but as you add layers of code, "not handled" may be a more appealing response than "broke my formula."

A clearer, though still simple, use of guards might be code that returns an absolute value. Yes, Erlang has a built-in function, abs/1, for this, but Example 3-3 shows how it works.

Example 3-3. Calculating absolute value with guards

```
-module(mathdemo).
-export([absolute_value/1]).

absolute_value(Number) when Number < 0  -> -Number;

absolute_value(Number) when Number == 0  -> 0;

absolute_value(Number) when Number > 0  -> Number.
```

When mathdemo:absolute_value is called with a negative (less than zero) argument, Erlang calls the first clause, which returns the negation of that negative argument, making it positive. When the argument equals (==) zero, Erlang calls the second clause, returning 0. Finally, when the argument is positive, Erlang calls the third clause, just returning the number. (The first two clauses have processed everything that isn't positive, so the guard on the last clause is unnecessary and will go away in Example 3-4.)

```
1> c(mathdemo).
{ok,mathdemo}
2> mathdemo:absolute_value(-20).
20
3> mathdemo:absolute_value(0).
0
4> mathdemo:absolute_value(20).
20
```

This may seem like an unwieldy way to calculate. Don't worry—Erlang has simpler logic switches you can use inside of functions. However, guards are critically important for choosing among function clauses, which will be especially useful as you start to work with recursion in Chapter 4.

Erlang runs through the function clauses in the order you list them, and stops at the first one that matches. If you find your information is heading to the wrong clause, you may want to reorder your clauses or fine-tune your guard conditions.

Also, when your guard clause is testing for just one value, you can easily switch to using pattern matching instead of a guard. This `absolute_value` function in Example 3-4 does the same thing as the one in Example 3-3.

Example 3-4. Calculating absolute value with guards and pattern matching

```
absolute_value(Number) when Number < 0  -> -Number;
absolute_value(0) -> 0;
absolute_value(Number) -> Number.
```

In this case, it's up to you whether you prefer the simpler form or preserving a parallel approach. You can also simplify the code by removing `absolute_value(0)` → `0;`, which is just a special case of `absolute_value(Number)` → `Number`, included for perhaps unnecessary clarity.

> You can also have multiple comparisons in a single guard. If you separate them with semicolons it works like an OR statement, succeeding if any of the comparisons succeed. If you separate them with commas, it works like an AND statement, and they all have to succeed for the guard to succeed.

Underscoring That You Don't Care

Guards let you specify more precise handling of incoming arguments. But sometimes you may actually want handling that is less precise. Not every argument is essential to every operation, especially when you start passing around complex data structures. You could create variables for arguments and then never use them, but you'll get warnings from the compiler (which suspects you must have made a mistake) and you may confuse other people using your code who are surprised to find your code cares about only half of the arguments they sent.

You might, for example, decide that you're not concerned with what planemo (for *planetary mass object*, including planets, dwarf planets, and moons) a user of your velocity function specifies and you're just going to use Earth's value for gravity. Then, you might write something like Example 3-5, from *ch03/ex3-underscore*.

Example 3-5. Declaring a variable and then ignoring it

```
-module(drop).
-export([fall_velocity/2]).

fall_velocity(Planemo, Distance) -> math:sqrt(2 * 9.8 * Distance).
```

This will compile, but you'll get a warning, and if you try to use it for, say, Mars, you'll get the wrong answer.

```
1> c(drop).
drop.erl:5: Warning: variable 'Planemo' is unused
{ok,drop}
2> drop:fall_velocity(mars, 20).
19.79898987322333
```

On Mars, that should be more like 12 than 19, so the compiler was right to scold you.

Sometimes, though, you don't actually care about some of the values that come to your function. In these cases, you can use a simple underscore (_). The underscore accomplishes two things: it tells the compiler not to bother you, and it tells anyone reading your code that you're not going to be using that argument. In fact, Erlang won't let you. You can try to assign values to the underscore, but Erlang won't give them back to you. It considers the underscore permanently unbound:

```
3> _ = 20.
20
4> _.
* 1: variable '_' is unbound
```

If you really wanted your code to be earth-centric and ignore any suggestions of other planemos, you could instead write something like Example 3-6.

Example 3-6. Deliberately ignoring an argument with an underscore

```
-module(drop2).
-export([fall_velocity/2]).

fall_velocity(_, Distance) -> math:sqrt(2 * 9.8 * Distance).
```

This time there will be no compiler warning, and anyone who looks at the code will know that first argument is useless.

```
5> c(drop2).
{ok,drop2}
6> drop2:fall_velocity(you_dont_care, 20).
19.79898987322333
```

You can use underscore multiple times to ignore multiple arguments. It matches anything for the pattern match, and never binds, so there's never a conflict.

You can also start variables with underscores—like _Planemo—and the compiler won't warn if you never use those variables. Those variables do get bound, and you can reference them later in your code if you change your mind. However, if you use the same variable name more than once in a set of arguments, even if the variable name starts with an underscore, you may get a warning from the compiler for trying to bind twice to the same name. (Pattern matching with underscore variables repeatedly, however, won't even produce a warning.)

Adding Structure: Tuples

Erlang's tuples let you combine multiple items into a single composite data type. This makes it easier to pass messages between components, letting you create your own complex data types as you need. Tuples can contain any kind of Erlang data, including numbers, atoms, other tuples, and the lists and strings you'll encounter in later chapters.

Tuples themselves are simple, a group of items surrounded by curly braces:

```
1> {earth, 20}.
{earth, 20}
```

Tuples might contain 1 item, or they might contain 100. Two to five seem typical (and useful, and readable). Often (but not always) an atom at the beginning of the tuple indicates what it's really for, providing an informal identifier of the complex information structure stored in the tuple.

Erlang includes rarely used built-in functions that give you access to the contents of a tuple on an item-by-item basis. You can retrieve the values of items with the element function, set values in a new tuple with the setelement function, and find out how many items are in a tuple with the tuple_size function.

```
2> Tuple = {earth, 20}.
{earth,20}
3> element(2, Tuple).
20
4> NewTuple = setelement(2, Tuple, 40).
{earth,40}
5> tuple_size(NewTuple).
2
```

If you can stick with pattern-matching tuples, however, you'll likely create more readable code.

Pattern Matching with Tuples

Tuples make it easy to package multiple arguments into a single container, and let the receiving function decide what to do with them. Pattern matching on tuples looks much like pattern matching on atoms, except that there is, of course, a pair of curly braces around each set of arguments. Example 3-7, which you'll find in *ch03/ex4-tuples*, demonstrates this.

Example 3-7. Encapsulating arguments in a tuple

```
-module(drop).
-export([fall_velocity/1]).

fall_velocity({earth, Distance}) -> math:sqrt(2 * 9.8 * Distance);

fall_velocity({moon, Distance}) -> math:sqrt(2 * 1.6 * Distance);

fall_velocity({mars, Distance}) -> math:sqrt(2 * 3.71 * Distance).
```

The arity changes: this version is `fall_velocity/1` instead of `fall_velocity/2` because the tuple counts as only one argument. The tuple version works much like the atom version but requires the extra curly braces when you call the function as well.

```
1> c(drop).
{ok,drop}
2> drop:fall_velocity({earth,20}).
19.79898987322333
3> drop:fall_velocity({moon,20}).
8.0
4> drop:fall_velocity({mars,20}).
12.181953866272849
```

Why would you use this form when it requires a bit of extra typing? Using tuples opens more possibilities. Other code could package different things into tuples—more arguments, different atoms, even functions created with `fun()`. Passing a single tuple rather than a pile of arguments gives Erlang much of its flexibility, especially when you get to passing messages between different processes.

Processing Tuples

There are many ways to process tuples, not just the simple pattern matching shown in Example 3-7. If you receive the tuple as a single variable, you can do many different things with it. A simple place to start is using the tuple as a pass through to a private version of the function. The last few parts of Example 3-8 may look familiar, as it's the same as the `fall_velocity/2` function in Example 3-2. (You can find this at *ch03/ex5-tuplesMore*.)

Example 3-8. Encapsulating arguments in a tuple and passing them to a private function

```
-module(drop).
-export([fall_velocity/1]).

fall_velocity({Planemo, Distance}) -> fall_velocity(Planemo, Distance).

fall_velocity(earth, Distance) when Distance >= 0  -> math:sqrt(2 * 9.8 * Distance);
fall_velocity(moon, Distance) when Distance >= 0 -> math:sqrt(2 * 1.6 * Distance);
fall_velocity(mars, Distance) when Distance >= 0 -> math:sqrt(2 * 3.71 * Distance).
```

The `-export` directive makes *only* `fall_velocity/1`, the tuple version, public. However, the `fall_velocity/2` function is available within the module. It's not especially necessary here, but this "make one version public, keep another version with different arity private" approach is common in situations where you want to make a function accessible but don't necessarily want its inner workings directly available.

If you call this function—the tuple version, so curly braces are necessary—`fall_velocity/1` calls the private `fall_velocity/2`, which returns the proper value to `fall_velocity/1`, which will return it to you. The results should look familiar:

```
1> c(drop).
{ok,drop}
2> drop:fall_velocity({earth,20}).
19.79898987322333
3> drop:fall_velocity({moon,20}).
8.0
4> drop:fall_velocity({mars,20}).
12.181953866272849
```

There are a few different ways to extract the data from the tuple. You could reference the components of the tuple by number using the built-in function `element`, which takes a numeric position and a tuple as its arguments. The first component of a tuple can be reached at position 1, the second at position 2, and so on.

```
fall_velocity(Where) -> fall_velocity(element(1,Where) , element(2,Where)).
```

You could also break things up a bit and do pattern matching after getting the variable:

```
fall_velocity(Where) ->
    {Planemo, Distance} = Where,
    fall_velocity(Planemo, Distance).
```

This function has more than one line. Note that actions are separated with commas, and that only the last line ends with a period. The result of that last line will be the value the function returns.

The pattern matching demonstrated here is a little different than in the previous examples. The function accepted a tuple as its argument and assigned it to the variable Where. (If Where is not a tuple, the function will fail with an error.) Extracting the contents of that tuple, since we know its structure, can be done with a pattern match inside the function. The Planemo and Distance variables will be bound to the values contained in the Where tuple, and can then be used in the call to fall_velocity/2.

 You can learn more about working with atoms, tuples, and pattern matching in Chapter 2 of *Erlang Programming* (O'Reilly); Chapter 3 of *Programming Erlang*, 2nd Edition (Pragmatic); Sections 2.2 and 2.4 of *Erlang and OTP in Action* (Manning); and Chapters 1 and 3 of *Learn You Some Erlang For Great Good!* (No Starch Press).

CHAPTER 4

Logic and Recursion

So far, Erlang seems logical but fairly simple. Pattern matching controls the flow through a program, and requests that match a form return certain responses. While this is enough to get many things done, there are times when you'll want more powerful options, especially as you start working with larger and more complicated data structures.

Logic Inside of Functions

Pattern matching and guards are powerful tools, but there are times when it's much easier to do some comparisons inside of a function clause instead of creating new functions. Erlang's designers agreed, and created two constructs for evaluating conditions inside of functions: the case expression and the less frequently used if expression.

The case construct lets you use pattern matching and guards inside of a function clause. It reads most clearly when a single value (or set of values) needs to be compared with multiple possibilities. The if construct evaluates only a series of guards, without pattern matching. The if construct tends to produce more readable code in situations where the multiple possibilities are specified by combinations of different values.

Both constructs return a value your code can capture.

Evaluating Cases

The case construct lets you perform pattern matching inside of your function clause. If you found the multiple function clauses of Example 3-2 hard to read, you might prefer to create a version that looks like Example 4-1, which you can find in *ch04/ex1-case*.

Example 4-1. Moving pattern matching inside the function

```
-module(drop).
-export([fall_velocity/2]).


fall_velocity(Planemo, Distance) when Distance >= 0  ->
  case Planemo of
    earth -> math:sqrt(2 * 9.8 * Distance);
    moon -> math:sqrt(2 * 1.6 * Distance);
    mars -> math:sqrt(2 * 3.71 * Distance)  % no closing period!
  end.
```

The `case` construct will compare the atom in `Planemo` to the values listed, going down the list in order. It won't process beyond the first match it finds. The `case` construct will return the result of different calculations based on which atom is used, and because the case construct returns the last value in the function clause, the function will return that value as well.

 You can use the underscore (_) for your pattern match if you want a choice that matches "everything else." However, you should always put that choice last—nothing that comes after that will ever be evaluated.

The results should look familiar:

```
1> c(drop).
{ok,drop}
2> drop:fall_velocity(earth,20).
19.79898987322333
3> drop:fall_velocity(moon,20).
8.0
4> drop:fall_velocity(mars,20).
12.181953866272849
5> drop:fall_velocity(mars,-20).
** exception error: no function clause matching
        drop:fall_velocity(mars,-20) (drop.erl, line 5)
```

The `case` construct switches among planemos, while the guard clause on the function definition keeps out negative distances, producing (rightly) the error on line 5. This way the guard needs to appear only once.

You can also use the return value from the `case` construct to reduce duplicate code and make the logic of your program clearer. In this case, the only difference between the calculations for `earth`, `moon`, and `mars` is a gravitational constant. Example 4-2, which you can find in *ch04/ex2-case*, shows how to make the case construct return the gravitational constant for use in a single calculation at the end.

Example 4-2. Using the return value of the case construct to clean up the function

```
-module(drop).
-export([fall_velocity/2]).


fall_velocity(Planemo, Distance) when Distance >= 0  ->
  Gravity = case Planemo of
    earth -> 9.8;
    moon ->  1.6;
    mars ->  3.71
  end,  % note comma - function isn't done yet

  math:sqrt(2 * Gravity * Distance).
```

This time, the `Gravity` variable is set to the return value of the `case` construct. Note the comma after the end. This function isn't done yet! Commas let you separate constructs inside of function declarations. The now more readable formula `math:sqrt(2 * Gravity * Distance).` is the last line of the function, and the value it produces will be the return value.

You can also use guards with a `case` statement, as shown, perhaps less than elegantly, in Example 4-3, which is in *ch04/ex3-case*. This example might make more sense if there were different planemos with different rules about distances.

Example 4-3. Moving guards into the case statement

```
-module(drop).
-export([fall_velocity/2]).

fall_velocity(Planemo, Distance)  ->
  Gravity = case Planemo of
    earth when Distance >= 0 ->  9.8;
    moon  when Distance >= 0 ->  1.6;
    mars  when Distance >= 0 ->  3.71
  end,  % note comma - function isn't done yet

  math:sqrt(2 * Gravity * Distance).
```

This produces results similar to those you saw earlier, except that the error message in response to line 3 changes from no function clause matching `drop:fall_velocity(mars,-20)` to no case clause matching `mars` in function `drop:fall_velocity/2`:

```
1> c(drop).
{ok,drop}
2> drop:fall_velocity(mars,20).
12.181953866272849
3> drop:fall_velocity(mars,-20).
** exception error: no case clause matching mars
      in function  drop:fall_velocity/2 (drop.erl, line 6)
```

The error is correct, in that the case construct is trying to match mars, but misleading because the problem isn't with mars but rather with the guard that's checking the Distance variable. If Erlang tells you that your case doesn't match but a match is obviously right there in front of you, check your guard statements.

If This, Then That

The if construct is broadly similar to the case statement, but without the pattern matching. This allows you to write a catch-all clause, a guard matching true at the end, and often makes it easier to express logic based on broader comparisons than simple matching.

Suppose, for example, that the precision of the fall_velocity function is too much. Instead of an actual speed you'd like to describe the speed produced by dropping from a tower of a given height. You can add an if construct that does that to the earlier code from Example 4-2, as shown in Example 4-4, in *ch04/ex4-if*.

Example 4-4. Adding an if construct to convert numbers into atoms

```
-module(drop).
-export([fall_velocity/2]).


fall_velocity(Planemo, Distance) when Distance >= 0  ->
  Gravity = case Planemo of
    earth -> 9.8;
    moon ->  1.6;
    mars ->  3.71
  end,

  Velocity = math:sqrt(2 * Gravity * Distance),

  if
    Velocity == 0 -> 'stable';
    Velocity < 5 -> 'slow';
    Velocity >= 5, Velocity < 10 -> 'moving';
    Velocity >= 10, Velocity < 20 -> 'fast';
    Velocity >= 20 -> 'speedy'
  end.
```

This time, the `if` construct returns a value (an atom describing the velocity) based on the many guards it includes. Because that value is the last thing returned within the function, that becomes the return value of the function.

 The commas in the `if` behave like the and operator.

The results are a little different from past trials:

```
1> c(drop).
{ok,drop}
2> drop:fall_velocity(earth,20).
fast
3> drop:fall_velocity(moon,20).
moving
4> drop:fall_velocity(mars,20).
fast
5> drop:fall_velocity(earth,30).
speedy
```

If you want to capture the value produced by the `if` construct and use it for something else, you can. Example 4-5, in *ch04/ex5-if*, sends a warning to standard output (in this case the Erlang shell) if you drop an object too fast.

Example 4-5. Sending an extra warning if the velocity is too high

```
-module(drop).
-export([fall_velocity/2]).

fall_velocity(Planemo, Distance) when Distance >= 0  ->
  Gravity = case Planemo of
    earth -> 9.8;
    moon ->  1.6;
    mars ->  3.71
  end,

  Velocity = math:sqrt(2 * Gravity * Distance),

  Description = if
    Velocity == 0 -> 'stable';
    Velocity < 5 -> 'slow';
    (Velocity >= 5) and (Velocity < 10) -> 'moving';
    (Velocity >= 10) and (Velocity < 20) -> 'fast';
    Velocity >= 20 -> 'speedy'
  end,

  if
```

```
  (Velocity > 40) -> io:format("Look out below!~n") ;
  true -> true
end,

Description.
```

The new (second) if clause checks the Velocity variable to see if it's above 40. If it is, it calls io:format, which creates a side effect: a message on the screen. However, every if must find some true statement or it will report an error if nothing matches. Here, you could add an explicit case matching when the Velocity is less than or equal to 40. But in many cases it won't matter. The true -> true line is a catch-all that returns true no matter what reaches it. After the if concludes, the single line Description. returns the contents of the Description variable from the function.

 The catch-all approach works in cases where you only want to test for a subset of cases among a complicated set of possibilities. In cases as simple as this example, however, it's probably cleaner to create a more explicit test.

The function produces an extra result—the message—when the distance is large enough (and the planemo's gravity strong enough) to produce a velocity faster than 40 meters per second:

```
1> c(drop).
{ok,drop}
2> drop:fall_velocity(earth,10).
fast
3> drop:fall_velocity(earth,200).
Look out below!
speedy
```

Variable Assignment in case and if Constructs

Every possible path created in a case or if statement has the opportunity to bind values to variables. This is usually a wonderful thing, but could result in unstable programs by assigning different variables in different clauses. This might look something like Example 4-6, which you can find in *ch04/ex6-broken*.

Example 4-6. A badly broken if construct

```
-module(broken).
-export([bad_if/1]).

bad_if(Test_val) ->

  if
```

```
   Test_val < 0 ->  X = 1;
   Test_val >= 0 -> Y = 2
 end,

 X+Y.
```

In theory, after the `case` or `if` is over, the program might crash because of unbound variables. However, Erlang won't let you get that far:

```
1> c(broken).
broken.erl:11: variable 'X' unsafe in 'if' (line 6)
broken.erl:11: variable 'Y' unsafe in 'if' (line 6)
error
```

The compilation errors turn up where your program actually uses the variables. The Erlang compiler double-checks to make sure the variables it's about to put to use are properly defined. It won't let you compile something that is broken.

You *can* bind variables in an `if` or `case` construct, but you have to define all of the variables in every single clause. If you're defining only one variable, it's also much cleaner to bind the return value of the `if` or `case` clause to a variable instead of defining that variable in every clause.

The Gentlest Side Effect: io:format

Up until Example 4-5, all of the Erlang examples you've seen focused on a single path through a group of functions. You put an argument or arguments in, and got a return value back. That approach is the cleanest way to do things: you can count on things that worked before to work again because there's no opportunity to muck up the system with leftovers of past processing.

Example 4-5 stepped outside of that model, creating a side effect that will linger after the function is complete. The side effect is just a message that appears in the shell (or in standard output when you start running Erlang outside of the shell). Applications that share information with multiple users or keep information around for longer than a brief processing cycle will need stronger side effects, like storing information in databases.

Erlang best practice suggests using side effects **only** when you really need to. An application that presents an interface to a database, for example, really will need to read and write that database. An application that interacts with users will need to put information on the screen (or other interface) so that users can figure out what they're expected to do.

Side effects are also extremely useful for tracing logic when you are first starting out. The simplest way to see what a program is doing, before you've learned how to use Erlang's built-in tracing and debugging tools for processes, is to have the program report its status at points you consider interesting. This is not a feature you want to leave in shipping code, but when you're getting started, it can give you an easily understandable window into your code's behavior.

The `io:format` function lets you send information to the console, or, when you're eventually running code outside of the console, to other places. For now, you'll just use it to send messages from the program to the console. Example 4-5 showed the simplest way to use `io:format`, just printing a message it takes in double quotes:

```
io:format("Look out below!~n") ;
```

The ~n represents a *newline*, telling the console to start any new messages it sends at the beginning of the next line. It makes your results look a bit neater.

The more typical way to use `io:format` includes two arguments: a double-quoted formatting string, and a list of values that can be included in the string. ~w lets you incorporate content without indentation or formatting. In this case (which you can see in *ch04/ex7-format*), it might look like the following:

```
io:format("Look out below!  ~w is too high.~n", [Distance]) ;
```

or:

```
io:format("Look out below!  ~w is too high on ~w.~n", [Distance, Planemo]) ;
```

`io:format/2` offers many formatting options beyond ~w and ~n. You'll encounter them in this book as they become necessary, but if you're impatient, there's a list in Appendix A. You may also want to explore the section on error logging in Chapter 9, if you find yourself using `io:format` for tasks that might be helped by more sophisticated logging tools.

Erlang flatly prohibits operations that could cause side effects in guard expressions. If side effects were allowed in guards, then any time a guard expression was evaluated—whether it returned true or false—the side effect would happen. `io:format` wouldn't likely do anything terrible, but these rules mean that it too is blocked from use in guard expressions.

Simple Recursion

Because variables can't change values, the main tool you'll use to repeat actions is recursion: having a function call itself until it's (hopefully) reached a conclusion. This can sound complicated, but it doesn't have to be.

There are two basic kinds of useful recursion. In some situations, you can count on the recursion to reach a natural end. The process runs out of items to work on, or reaches a natural limit. In other situations, there is no natural end, and you need to keep track of the result so the process will end. If you can master these two basic forms, you'll be able to create many more complex variations.

 There is a third form in which the recursive calls never reach an end. This is called an *infinite loop*, and is best known as an error you'll want to avoid. As you'll see in Chapter 8, though, even infinite loops can be useful.

Counting Down

The simplest model of recursion with a natural limit is a countdown, like the one used for rockets. You start with a large number, and count down to zero. When you reach zero, you're done (and the rocket takes off, if there is one).

To implement this in Erlang, you'll pass a starting number to an Erlang function. If the number is greater than zero, it will then announce the number and call itself with the number minus one as the argument. If the number is zero (or less), it will announce blastoff! and end. Example 4-7, found in *ch04/ex8-countdown*, shows one way to do this.

Example 4-7. Counting down

```
-module(count).
-export([countdown/1]).


countdown(From) when From > 0 ->
   io:format("~w!~n", [From]),
   countdown(From-1);

countdown(From) ->
   io:format("blastoff!~n").
```

The last clause could have a guard—when From =< 0—but it would be useful only to make clear when the blastoff happens to human readers. Unnecessary guard clauses may lead to weird errors, so brevity is probably the best option here, though you'll get a warning that From is unused in the final clause. Here's a test run:

```
1> c(count).
count.erl:9: Warning: variable 'From' is unused
{ok,count}
2> count:countdown(2).
2!
1!
blastoff!
ok
```

The first time through, Erlang chose the first clause of countdown(From), passing it a value of 2. That clause printed 2, plus an exclamation point and a newline, and then it called the countdown function again, passing it a value of 1. That triggered the first clause again. It printed 1, plus an exclamation point and a newline, and then it called the countdown function again—this time passing it a value of 0.

The value of 0 triggered the second clause, which printed blastoff! and ended. After running three values through the same set of code, the function comes to a neat conclusion.

 You could also implement this conclusion with an if statement inside a single countdown(From) function clause, but this construction is unusual in Erlang. I find guards more readable in these cases, but you may see things differently.

Counting Up

Counting up is trickier because there's no natural endpoint, so you can't model your code on Example 4-7. Erlang's single-assignment approach to variables rules out some approaches, but one way to make this work uses an *accumulator*. An accumulator is an extra argument that keeps track of the current result of past work, passing it back into a recursive function. (You can have more than one accumulator argument if you need, though one is often sufficient.) Example 4-8, which you can find in *ch04/ex9-countup*, shows how to add a countup function to the count module, which lets Erlang count up to a number.

Example 4-8. Counting up

```
-module(count).
-export([countdown/1, countup/1]).

countup(Limit) ->
  countup(1, Limit).

countup(Count, Limit) when Count =< Limit ->
    io:format("~w!~n", [Count]),
    countup(Count+1, Limit);

countup(Count, Limit) ->
    io:format("Finished.~n").

...
```

It produces results such as the following:

```
1> c(count).
{ok,count}
2> count:countup(2).
1!
2!
Finished.
ok
```

The export directive makes the countup/1 function visible (as well as the earlier countdown/1, which you'll find in the sample code).

The countup/2 function, which does most of the work, remains private, not exported. This isn't mandatory. You might make it public if you wanted to support counting between arbitrary values, but keeping it private is common Erlang practice. Keeping the recursive internal functions private makes it less likely that someone will misuse them for purposes they're not well-suited to. In this case, it doesn't matter at all, but it can make a big difference in other more complex situations, especially when data is modified.

When you call countup/1, it calls countup/2 with an argument of 1 (for the current count) and the Limit value you provided for the upper limit.

If the current count is less than or equal to the upper limit, the first clause of the countup/2 function reports the current Count value with io:format. Then it calls itself again, increasing the Count by one but leaving the Limit alone.

If the current count is greater than the upper limit, it fails the guard on the first clause, so the second clause kicks in, reports "Finished," and is done.

 The guards here are sufficient to avoid infinite loops. You can enter zero, negative numbers, or decimals as arguments to countup/1 and it will terminate neatly. You can get into serious trouble, however, if your termination test relies on == or =:= for a more exact comparison rather than >= or =< for a rough comparison.

Recursing with Return Values

The counting examples are simple—they demonstrate how recursion works, but just discard the return values. There are return values—the io:format calls return the atom ok—but they aren't of much use. More typically, a recursive function call will make use of the return value.

A classic recursive call calculates factorials. A factorial is the product of all positive integers equal to or less than the argument. The factorial of 1 is 1; 1 by itself yields 1.

The factorial of 2 is 2; 2 × 1 yields 2. It starts to get interesting at 3, where 3 × 2 × 1 is 6. At 4, 4 × 3 × 2 × 1 is 24, and the results get larger rapidly with larger arguments.

But there's a pattern here. You can calculate any factorial by multiplying the integer by the factorial of one less. That makes it a perfect case for using recursion, using the results of smaller integers to calculate the larger ones. This approach is similar to the countdown logic, but instead of just counting, the program collects calculated results. That could look like Example 4-9, which you'll find in *ch04/ex10-factorial-down*.

Example 4-9. A factorial written with the counting-down approach

```
-module(fact).
-export([factorial/1]).

factorial(N) when N > 1->
  N * factorial(N-1);

factorial(N) when N =< 1 ->
  1.
```

The first clause of `factorial` uses the pattern previously described. The first clause, used for numbers above one, returns a value that is the number N times the factorial of the next integer down. The second clause returns the value 1 when it reaches 1. Using `=<` in that comparison, rather than `==`, gives the function more resilience against noninteger or negative arguments, though the answers it returns aren't quite right: factorials really only work for integers of 1 or higher. The results are as previously suggested:

```
1> c(fact).
{ok,fact}
2> fact:factorial(1).
1
3> fact:factorial(3).
6
4> fact:factorial(4).
24
5> fact:factorial(40).
815915283247897734345611269596115894272000000000
```

This works, but it may not be clear why it works. Yes, the function counts down and collects the values, but if you want to see the mechanism, you need to add some `io:format` calls into the code, as shown in Example 4-10. (You can find this at *ch04/ex10-factorial-down-instrumented*.)

Example 4-10. Looking into the factorial recursion calls

```
-module(fact).
-export([factorial/1]).
```

```
factorial(N) when N > 1->
  io:format("Calling from ~w.~n", [N]),
  Result = N * factorial(N-1),
  io:format("~w yields ~w.~n", [N, Result]),
  Result;

factorial(N) when N =< 1 ->
  io:format("Calling from 1.~n"),
  io:format("1 yields 1.~n"),
  1.
```

There's a bit more overhead here. Presenting the result of the recursive call and still returning that value to the next recursive call requires storing it in a variable, here called Result. The io:format call makes visible which value produced the result. Then, because the last value expression in a function clause is the return value, Result appears again. The second clause for 1 is similar, except that it can report simply that 1 yields 1. because it always will.

When you compile this and run it, you'll see something such as the following:

```
7> fact:factorial(4).
Calling from 4.
Calling from 3.
Calling from 2.
Calling from 1.
1 yields 1.
2 yields 2.
3 yields 6.
4 yields 24.
24
```

Although the calls count down the values, as the logic would suggest, the messages about results don't appear until the countdown is complete, and then they all appear in order, counting up.

The reason this happens is that the function calls don't return values until the countdown is complete. Until then, the Erlang runtime builds a stack of frames corresponding to the function calls. You can think of the frames as paused versions of the function logic, waiting for an answer to come back. Once the call with an argument of 1 returns a simple value, not calling any further, Erlang can unwind those frames and calculate the Result. That unwinding presents the results—"X yields Y"—in the order that the frames unwind.

That "unwinding" also means that the code in Examples 4-9 and 4-10 is not *tail recursive*. When Erlang encounters code that ends with a simple recursive call, it can optimize the handling to avoid keeping that stack of calls around. This probably doesn't matter for a one-time calculation, but it makes a huge difference when you write code that will stay running for a long time.

You can achieve tail recursion for factorials by applying the counting-up approach to factorials. You'll get the same results (at least for integer values), but the calculations will work a little differently, as shown in Example 4-11, at *ch04/ex12-factorial-up*.

Example 4-11. A factorial written with the counting-up approach

```
-module(fact).
-export([factorial/1]).


factorial(N) ->
  factorial(1, N, 1).

factorial(Current, N, Result) when Current =< N ->
    NewResult = Result*Current,
    io:format("~w yields ~w!~n", [Current, NewResult]),
    factorial(Current+1, N, NewResult);

factorial(Current, N, Result) ->
    io:format("Finished.~n"),
    Result.
```

As in the counting-up example, the main function call, here `factorial/1`, calls a private function, `factorial/3`. In this case, there are two accumulators. `Current` stores the current position in the count, whereas `Result` is the answer from the previous multiplication. When the value of `Current` climbs past the limiting value `N`, the first guard fails, the second clause is invoked, and the function is finished and returns the `Result`. (You'll get a compilation warning because the final clause doesn't use the accumulator variables `Current` or `N`. You can ignore it.)

Because `factorial/3`'s last call in the recursive section is to itself, without any complications to track, it is tail recursive. That allows Erlang to minimize the amount of information it has to keep around while the calls all happen.

The calculation produces the same results, but does the math in a different order:

```
9> fact:factorial(4).
1 yields 1!
2 yields 2!
3 yields 6!
4 yields 24!
Finished.
24
```

Although the code is tracking more values, the Erlang runtime has less to do. When it finally hits the final result, there's no further calculation needed. That result is the result, and it passes back through to the original call. This also makes it easier to structure the `io:format` calls. If you remove them or comment them out, the rest of the code stays the same.

You can also achieve tail recursion while counting down, without using a counter (Example 4-12).

Example 4-12. A concise factorial that counts down

```
-module(fact).
-export([factorial/1]).

factorial(N) -> factorial(N,1).
factorial(N, Result) when N > 1 ->
  factorial(N-1, N*Result);
factorial(N, Result) when N =< 1 ->
  Result.
```

 You can learn more about working with logical flow and recursion in Chapter 3 of *Erlang Programming* (O'Reilly); Chapter 4 of *Programming Erlang*, 2nd Edition (Pragmatic); Sections 2.6 and 2.15 of *Erlang and OTP in Action* (Manning); and Chapters 3 and 5 of *Learn You Some Erlang For Great Good!* (No Starch Press).

CHAPTER 5

Communicating with Humans

Erlang's origins in telecom switching have left it with a fairly minimal set of tools for communicating with people, but there's enough there to do worthwhile things. You've already used some of it (io:format/1 and io:format/2), but there are more pieces you'll want to learn to handle communications with people and sometimes with other applications. At the very least, this chapter will let you build more convenient interfaces for testing your code than calling functions from the Erlang shell.

 If you're feeling completely excited about the recursion you learned in Chapter 4, you may want to jump ahead to Chapter 6, where that recursion will once again be front and center.

Strings

Atoms are great for sending messages within a program, even messages that the programmer can remember, but they're not really designed for communicating outside of the context of Erlang processes. If you need to assemble sentences or even presenting information, you'll want something more flexible. Strings, sequences of characters, are the structure you need. You've already used strings a little bit, as the double-quoted arguments to io:format in Chapter 4:

```
io:format("Look out below!~n") ;
```

The double-quoted content (Look out below!~n) is a string. A string is a sequence of characters. If you want to include a double-quote within the string, you can escape it with a backslash, like \". To include a backslash, you have to use \\, and Appendix A includes a complete list of escapes and other options. If you create a string in the shell, Erlang will report back the string *with* the escapes. To see what it is meant to contain, use `io:format`:

```
1> X = "Quote - \" in a string. \n  Backslash, too: \\ . \n".
"Quote - \" in a string. \n  Backslash, too: \\ ."
2> io:format(X).
Quote -  " in a string.
  Backslash, too: \ .
ok
```

If you start entering a string and don't close the quotes, when you press Enter, the Erlang shell will just give you a new line with the same number. This lets you include newlines in strings, but it can be very confusing. If you think you're stuck, usually entering ". will get you out of it.

Erlang development hasn't focused heavily on text historically, but if your programs involve sharing information with humans, you'll want to get familiar with how to get information into and out of strings. This is an area where you may want to spend a fair amount of time in the shell playing with different tools.

Technically, strings don't really exist as a type in Erlang because strings are lists of characters. Thinking about strings as lists of characters, however, is useful in only a few situations, typically where you want to process a string from start to end. You'll learn about lists in Chapter 6, and the code in this chapter will have to use a list built-in function, but for now you should just think about string operations rather than lists.

The simplest approach, usually, is concatenation, where you combine two strings into one. Erlang offers two easy ways to do this. The first uses the ++ operator:

```
1> "erl" ++ "ang".
"erlang"
2> A="ang".
"ang"
3> "erl" ++ A.
"erlang"
```

The other approach uses an explicit `string:concat/2` function:

```
4> string:concat("erl", "ang").
"erlang"
5> N="ang".
"ang"
6> string:concat("erl", N).
"erlang"
```

The ++ operator is usually more convenient because it lets you work with more than two arguments without nesting functions.

Erlang has a shortcut where you can concatenate two strings just by putting them next to each other: `"erl" "ang"` will end up as `"erlang"`. However, if you try to mix variables into that, you'll get a syntax error. This shortcut is of limited value except maybe when you're cutting and pasting quoted values as you're writing your code, and doesn't work in every context.

Erlang also offers three options for comparing string equality, the `==` operator, the `=:=` (exact equality) operator, and a `string:equal/2` function. The `==` operator is generally the simplest for this, though the others produce the same results:

```
7> "erl" == "erl".
true
8> "erl" == "ang".
false
9> G ="ang".
"ang"
10> G == "ang".
true
```

Erlang doesn't offer functions for changing strings in place, as that would work badly with a model where variable contents don't change. However, it does offer a set of functions for finding content in strings and dividing or padding those strings, which together let you extract information from a string (or multiple strings) and recombine it into a new string.

If you want to do more with your strings, you should definitely explore the documentation for the `string` and `re` (regular expressions) Erlang modules. If the strings you want to work with represent file or directory names, definitely explore the `filename` module. If you need to perform Unicode-encoding conversion on Erlang strings, you'll also want to explore the `unicode` module. (By default, Erlang represents characters using UTF-8 values.)

I wrote a single wrapper module that assembles Erlang's tools for working with strings into one place. For more, visit *https://github.com/simonstl/erlang-simple-string*.

Asking Users for Information

Many Erlang applications run kind of like wholesalers—in the background, providing goods and services to retailers who interact directly with users. Sometimes, however, it's nice to have a direct interface to code that is a little more customized than the Erlang console. You probably won't write many Erlang applications whose primary interface is the command line, but you may find that interface very useful when you first try out your code. (Odds are good that if you're working with Erlang, you don't mind using a command-line interface, either.)

You *can* mix input and output with your program logic, but for this kind of simple facade, it probably makes better sense to put input in a separate module. In this case, the `ask` module will work with the `drop` module from Example 3-8.

Erlang's `io` functions for input have a variety of strange interactions with the Erlang shell, as discussed in the following section. You will have better luck working with them in other contexts.

Gathering Terms

The simplest way to build an interface—an interface probably just for programmers —is to create a way for users to enter Erlang terms using `io:read/1`. This lets users enter a complete Erlang term—an atom, number, or tuple, for example. An initial version of this might look like Example 5-1, which you can find in *ch05/ex1-ask*.

Example 5-1. Asking the user for an Erlang term

```
-module(ask).
-export([term/0]).

term() ->
  Input = io:read("What {planemo, distance} ? >>"),
  Term = element(2,Input),
  drop:fall_velocity(Term).
```

The `Input` variable will be set by the call to `io:read/1`, getting an Erlang term. If all goes well, it will contain a tuple like `{ok,{mars,20}}`, where the first value is `ok` and the second value of the tuple is the term the user entered. Extracting that value—in this case a tuple—requires a call to the `element/2` method. Finally, the code calls the `drop:fall_velocity` method with that value.

If you wanted, you could cram that all into one line as `term()` `-> drop:fall_velocity(element(2,io:read("What {planemo, distance} ? >>")))`., but that's both hard to read and hard to modify.

For your own use, this could be perfectly fine. A simple session might look like the following:

```
1> c(drop).
{ok,drop}
2> c(ask).
{ok,ask}
3> ask:term().
What {planemo, distance} ? >>{mars,20}.
12.181953866272849
```

If you leave off the period at the end of the term, Erlang will repeat the prompt but not show where you were, trusting you to read the line above. Also, the things you enter at an `io:read/1` prompt become part of the console's command history, and you can repeat them with the up arrow. (These issues are interactions with the Erlang shell, not issues with the function itself.)

Things can get weird quickly, however, if the user enters unexpected terms—a number instead of a tuple, say—or broken terms, with bad syntax:

```
4> ask:term().
What {planemo, distance} ? >>20.
** exception error: no function clause matching
          drop:fall_velocity(20) (drop.erl, line 4)
5> ask:term().
What {planemo, distance} ? >>.
** exception error: no function clause matching
            drop:fall_velocity({1,erl_parse,
            ["syntax error before: ","'.'"]}) (drop.erl, line 4)
```

In both cases, passing the extracted `Term` directly to `fall_velocity/1` is a bad idea. In the first case, it's because `fall_velocity/1` expects a tuple, not a bare number. In the second case, `fall_velocity/1` has a similar problem, but it's being sent an error message, not a term it can process. Example 5-2, in *ch05/ex2-ask*, shows a better way to handle these kinds of problems. It gives the user a direct error message when it encounters the wrong type of information or broken information. (It also uses pattern matching instead of `element/2`.)

Example 5-2. Asking the user for an Erlang term and handling bad results

```
-module(ask).
-export([term/0]).
```

```
term() ->
  Input = io:read("What {planemo, distance} ? >>"),
  process_term(Input).

process_term({ok, Term}) when is_tuple(Term) -> drop:fall_velocity(Term);

process_term({ok, _}) -> io:format("You must enter a tuple.~n");

process_term({error, _}) -> io:format("You must enter a tuple with correct syntax.~n").
```

This doesn't solve every possible problem. Users could still enter tuples with the wrong content, and drop:fall_velocity will report an error. Chapter 9 will explore how to address that problem in much greater detail.

When you go to the trouble of building this kind of interface, however, it's probably not because typing ask:term() is shorter than typing drop:fall_velocity. Odds are good that you want to try a number of values and possibilities, so you want the question repeated. Example 5-3, in *ch05/ex3-ask*, presents the result of a (correctly formatted) call to the user and then calls term() again, setting up a recursive loop. (It also offers a nice way to exit the loop.)

Example 5-3. Asking the user for an Erlang term and handling bad results

```
-module(ask).
-export([term/0]).

term() ->
  Input = io:read("What {planemo, distance} ? >>"),
  process_term(Input).

process_term({ok, Term}) when is_tuple(Term) ->
  Velocity = drop:fall_velocity(Term),
  io:format("Yields ~w. ~n",[Velocity]),
  term();

process_term({ok, quit}) ->
  io:format("Goodbye.~n");
  % does not call term() again

process_term({ok, _}) ->
  io:format("You must enter a tuple.~n"),
  term();

process_term({error, _}) ->
  io:format("You must enter a tuple with correct syntax.~n"),
  term().
```

When you compile the ask module and call ask:term/0, you'll see the question repeated as long as you keep entering appropriate tuples. To break out of that loop, just enter the atom quit followed by a period.

```
6> c(ask).
{ok,ask}
7> ask:term().
What {planet, distance} ? >>{mars,20}.
Yields 12.181953866272849.
What {planet, distance} ? >>20.
You must enter a tuple.
What {planet, distance} ? >>quit.
Goodbye.
ok
```

Gathering Characters

The io:get_chars/2 function will let you get just a few characters from the user. This would be convenient if, for example, you have a list of options. Present the options to the user, and wait for a response. In this example, the list of planemos is the option, and they're easy to number 1 through 3, as shown in the code for Example 5-4, which you can find at *ch05/ex4-ask*. That means you just need a single character response.

Example 5-4. Presenting a menu and waiting for a single-character response

```
-module(ask).
-export([chars/0]).

chars() ->
  io:format("Which planemo are you on?~n"),
  io:format(" 1. Earth ~n"),
  io:format(" 2. Earth's Moon~n"),
  io:format(" 3. Mars~n"),
  io:get_chars("Which? > ",1).
```

Most of that is presenting the menu, and you could combine all of those io:format/1 calls into a single call if you wanted. The key piece is the io:get_chars/2 call at the end. The first argument is a prompt, and the second is the number of characters you want returned. The function still lets users enter whatever they want until they press Enter, but it will tell you only the first of however many characters you specified.

```
1> c(ask).
{ok,ask}
2> ask:chars().
Which planemo are you on?
 1. Earth
 2. Earth's Moon
 3. Mars
Which? > 3
```

```
"3"
3>
3>
```

After the user hits Enter, the `io:get_chars` function returns the string "3", the character the user entered. However, as you can tell by the duplicated command prompt, the Enter still gets reported to the Erlang shell. This can get stranger if users enter more content than is needed:

```
4> ask:chars().
Which planemo are you on?
  1. Earth
  2. Earth's Moon
  3. Mars
Which? > 222222
"2"
5> 22222
5>
```

There may be times when `io:get_chars` is exactly what you want, but odds are good, at least when working within the shell, that you'll get cleaner results by taking in a complete line of user input and picking what you want from it.

Reading Lines of Text

Erlang offers a few different functions that pause to request information from users. The `io:get_line/1` function waits for the user to enter a complete line of text terminated by a newline. You can then process the line to extract the information you want, and nothing will be left in the buffer. Example 5-5, in *ch05/ex5-ask*, shows how this could work, though extracting the information is somewhat more complicated than I would like.

Example 5-5. Collecting user responses a line at a time

```
-module(ask).
-export([line/0]).

line() ->
  Planemo = get_planemo(),
  Distance = get_distance(),
  drop:fall_velocity({Planemo, Distance}).


get_planemo() ->
  io:format("Where are you?~n"),
  io:format(" 1. Earth ~n"),
  io:format(" 2. Earth's Moon~n"),
  io:format(" 3. Mars~n"),
  Answer = io:get_line("Which? > "),
```

```
    Value = hd(Answer),
    char_to_planemo(Value).

char_to_planemo(Char) ->
  if
    [Char] == "1" -> earth;
    Char == $2 -> moon;
    Char == 51 -> mars
  end.

get_distance() ->
  Input = io:get_line("How far? (meters) > "),
  Value = string:strip(Input, right, $\n),
  {Distance, _} = string:to_integer(Value),
  Distance.
```

To clarify the code, the line/0 function just calls three other functions. It calls get_planemo/0 to present a menu to the user and get a reply, and it similarly calls get_distance/0 to ask the user the distance of the fall. Then it calls drop:fall_velocity/1 to return the velocity at which a frictionless object will hit the ground when dropped from that height at that location.

The get_planemo/0 function is a combination of io:format/1 calls to present information and an io:get_line/1 call to retrieve information from the user. Unlike io:get_chars/1, io:get_line/1 returns the entire value the user entered, including the newline, and leaves nothing in the buffer.

```
get_planemo() ->
  io:format("Where are you?~n"),
  io:format(" 1. Earth ~n"),
  io:format(" 2. Earth's Moon~n"),
  io:format(" 3. Mars~n"),
  Answer = io:get_line("Which? > "),

  Character = hd(Answer),
  char_to_planemo(Character).
```

The last two lines are the actual string processing. The only piece of the response that matters to this application is the first character of the string. The easy way to grab that is with the built-in function hd/1, which pulls the first item from a string or list.

 Because strings are really lists of numbers, you could instead call lists:nth(1, Answer). The first argument, 1, is the position you want to retrieve, and the second argument, Answer, is the list, in this case a string, from which you want to retrieve it. For this function, the first character in an Erlang string is in position 1, not 0 as in many other languages. That makes the function name nth make sense when it's time to retrieve the 4th, 5th, 6th, and so on values.

The `drop:fall_velocity/1` function won't know what to do with a planemo listed as 1, 2, or 3; it expects an atom of `earth`, `moon`, or `mars`. The `get_planemo/0` function concludes by returning the value of that conversion, performed by the `char_to_planemo/1` function:

```
char_to_planemo(Char) ->
  if
    [Char] == "1" -> earth;
    Char == $2 -> moon;
    Char == 51 -> mars
  end.
```

The `if` statement shows three different ways of testing the character. If you prefer to evaluate the character as text, you can put square brackets around it and compare it to a string, like `"1"` here. You can also test against Erlang's character notation, in which `$2` is the value for the character two. Finally, if you're comfortable with character values, you can compare it to those values, like `51`, which corresponds to the character 3. The atom returned by the case statement will be returned to the `get_planemo/0` function, which will in turn return it to the `line/0` function for use in the calculation.

You could also rewrite that function to skip the `case` statement and just use pattern matching:

```
char_to_planemo($1) -> earth;
char_to_planemo($2) -> moon;
char_to_planemo($3) -> mars.
```

Erlang's character notation understands Unicode as well. If you try $☃, the Unicode Snowman, Erlang will understand that it is character 9731, hex 2603. It also understands Emoji characters from Unicode's Astral Plane, which are often difficult for simple Unicode implementations.

Getting the distance is somewhat easier:

```
get_distance() ->
  Input = io:get_line("How far? (meters) > "),
  Value = string:strip(Input, right, $\n),
  {Distance, _} = string:to_integer(Value),
  Distance.
```

The `Input` variable collects the user's response to the question "How far?", and `Value` strips extra noise out of that response. The `string:to_integer/1` function extracts an integer from `Value`. The pattern match on the left grabs the first piece of the tuple it returns, which is the integer, while the underscore discards the rest of what it sends, which is anything else on the line. That will include the newline, but also any decimal part users enter. You could use `string:to_float/1` for more precision, but that won't accept an integer. Using `string:to_integer/1` isn't perfect, but for these purposes it's probably acceptable.

 It isn't necessary for this conversion, but if you *just* want to strip newlines out of user responses, you can use `string:strip(Input, right, $\n)`, where `Input` is what just came from the user.

A sample run demonstrates that this code produces the right results given the right input:

```
1> c(ask).
{ok,ask}
2> ask:line().
Where are you?
 1. Earth
 2. Earth's Moon
 3. Mars
Which? > 1
How far? (meters) > 20
19.79898987322333
3> ask:line().
Where are you?
 1. Earth
 2. Earth's Moon
 3. Mars
Which? > 2
How far? > 20
8.0
```

Chapter 9 will return to this code, looking at better ways to handle the errors users can provoke by entering unexpected answers.

Strings are not Erlang's strongest suit, but it has the facilities to make pretty much anything you need work. As you read the next two chapters on lists, remember that strings are actually lists of characters underneath, and you can use any of the list tools on strings.

 You can learn more about working with strings in Chapter 2 of *Erlang Programming* (O'Reilly); Sections 3.8 and 8.8 of *Programming Erlang*, 2nd Edition (Pragmatic); Section 2.2.6 of *Erlang and OTP in Action* (Manning); and Chapter 1 of *Learn You Some Erlang For Great Good!* (No Starch Press).

CHAPTER 6

Lists

Erlang is great at handling lists, long series of values. List processing makes it easy to see the value of recursion, and offers opportunities to get a lot of work done for very little effort.

List Basics

An Erlang list is an ordered set of elements. Generally you will process a list in order, from the first item (the *head*) to the last item, though there are times when you may want to grab a particular item from the list. Erlang also provides built-in functions for manipulating lists when you don't want to go through the entire sequence.

Erlang syntax encloses lists in square brackets and separates elements with commas. A list of numbers might look like the following:

```
[1,2,4,8,16,32]
```

The elements can be of any type, including numbers, atoms, tuples, strings, and other lists. When you're starting out, it's definitely easiest to work with lists that contain only a single type of element, rather than mixing all the possibilities, but Erlang itself has no such constraint. There is also no limit on the number of items a list can contain, though eventually you may find practical limits of memory.

You can pattern match with lists just as you can with other Erlang data structures:

```
1> [1,X,4,Y] = [1,2,4,8].
[1,2,4,8]
2> X.
2
3> Y.
8
```

While it's possible to use lists instead of tuples, your code will make more sense if you use tuples to handle data structures containing various kinds of data in a known structure, and lists to handle data structures containing less varied data in unknown quantities. (Tuples are expected to come in a certain order and can also contain lists, so if you have a data structure that's mostly known except for an expanding part or two, including a list inside of a tuple can be a workable solution.)

Lists can contain lists, and sometimes this can produce surprising results. If, for example, you want to add a list to a list, you may end up with more levels of list than you planned:

```
4> Insert=[2,4,8].
[2,4,8]
5> Full = [1, Insert, 16, 32].
[1,[2,4,8],16,32]
```

You can fix that (if you want to) with the `lists:flatten/1` function:

```
6> Neat = lists:flatten(Full).
[1,2,4,8,16,32]
```

This also means that if you want to append lists, you need to decide whether you're creating a list of lists or a single list containing the contents of the component lists. To create a list of lists, you just put lists into lists.

```
7> A = [1,2,4].
[1,2,4]
8> B = [8,16,32].
[8,16,32]
9> ListOfLists = [A,B].
[[1,2,4],[8,16,32]]
```

To create a single list from multiple lists, you can use the `lists:append/2` function or the equivalent ++ operator.

```
10> Combined1 = lists:append(A,B).
[1,2,4,8,16,32]
11> Combined2 = A ++ B.
[1,2,4,8,16,32]
```

Both produce the same result: a combined and flattened list.

The ++ operator is right associative, which can change the order of the resulting list when you append multiple lists.

If you have a set of lists you'd like combined, you can use the `lists:append/1` function, which takes a list of lists as its argument and returns a single list containing their contents:

```
12> C = [64,128,256].
[64,128,256]
13> Combined4 = lists:append([A,B,C]).
[1,2,4,8,16,32,64,128,256]
```

If you want to generate a list of sequential integers (or characters), the `lists:seq/2` function is handy. Its arguments are the start and end of the list values. For example, `lists:seq(-2,8)` produces `[-2,-1,0,1,2,3,4,5,6,7,8]`, and `lists:seq($A,$z)` produces the string (list) `"ABCDEFGHIJKLMNOPQRSTUVWXYZ[\\]^_`abcdefghijklmnopqrstuvwxyz"`.

Splitting Lists into Heads and Tails

Lists are a convenient way to hold piles of similar data, but their great strength in Erlang is the way they make it easy to do recursion. Lists are a natural fit for the "counting down" style of logic explored in Chapter 4: you can run through a list until you run out of items. In many languages, running through a list means finding out how many items it contains and going through them sequentially. Erlang takes a different approach, letting you process the first item in a list, the *head*, while extracting the rest of the list, the *tail*, so that you can pass it to another call recursively.

To extract the head and the tail, you use pattern matching, with a special form of the list syntax on the left:

```
[Head | Tail] = [1,2,4].
```

The two variables separated by a vertical bar (|), or cons, short for list constructor, will be bound to the head and tail of the list on the right. In the console, Erlang will just report the contents of the right side of the expression, not the fragments created by the pattern match, but if you work through a list you can see the results:

```
1> List = [1,2,4].
[1,2,4]
2> [H1 | T1] = List.
[1,2,4]
3> H1.
1
4> T1.
[2,4]
5> [H2 | T2] = T1.
[2,4]
6> H2.
2
```

```
7> T2.
[4]
8> [H3 | T3] = T2.
[4]
9> H3.
4
10> T3.
[]
11> [H4 | T4] = T3.
** exception error: no match of right-hand side value []
```

Line 2 breaks the initial list into two smaller pieces. H1 will contain the first item of the List, whereas T1 will contain a list that has everything *except* the first element. Line 5 repeats the process on the smaller list, breaking T1 into an H2 and a T2. This time T2 is still a list, as shown on line 7, but contains only one item. Line 8 breaks that single-item list again, putting the value into H3 and an *empty* list into T3.

What happens when you try to split an empty list, as shown on line 11? Erlang reports an error, "no match…". Fortunately, this does not mean that recursion on lists is doomed to produce errors. That lack of a match will naturally stop the recursive process, which is probably what you want.

 Head and tail work only move forward through a list. If order matters and you really need to go through a list backwards, you'll need to use the lists:reverse function and then walk through the reversed list.

Processing List Content

The head and tail notation was built for recursive processing. Using this approach, a list arrives as an argument and is then passed to another (usually private) function with an accumulator argument. A simple case might perform a calculation on the contents of the list. Example 6-1, in *ch06/ex1-product*, shows this pattern in use, multiplying the values of a list together.

Example 6-1. Calculating the product of values in a list

```
-module(overall).
-export([product/1]).

product([]) -> 0; % in case the list is empty, return zero
product(List) -> product(List,1).

product([], Product) -> Product;  % when list empty, stop, report

product([Head|Tail], Product) -> product(Tail, Product * Head).
```

In this module, the product/1 function is the gateway, passing the list (if the list has content) plus an accumulator to product/2, which does the real work. If you wanted to test the arriving list to make sure it meets your expectations, it probably makes the most sense to do that work in product/1, and let product/2 focus on recursive processing.

 Is the product of an empty list really zero? It might make more sense for an empty list to fail and produce a crash. Erlang's "let it crash" philosophy is, as you'll see later, pretty calm about such things. In the long run, you'll have to decide which cases are better left to crash and which aren't.

The product/2 function has two clauses. The first matches the empty list, and will get called at the end of the recursive process when there are no more entries to process, or if the list arrives empty. It returns its second argument, the accumulator.

If the arriving list is not empty, the second clause goes to work. First, the pattern match ([Head|Tail]) splits off the first value of the list from the rest of the list. Next, it calls product/2 again, with the remaining (if any) portion of the list and a new accumulator that is multiplied by the value of the first entry in the list. The result will be the product of the values included in the list:

```
1> c(overall).
{ok,overall}
2> overall:product([1,2,3,5]).
30
```

That went smoothly, but what happened? After product/1 called product/2, it made five iterations over the list, concluding with an empty list, as shown in Table 6-1.

Table 6-1. Recursive processing of a simple list in product/2

Arriving List	Arriving Product	Head	Tail
[1,2,3,5]	1	1	[2,3,5]
[2,3,5]	1 (1*1)	2	[3,5]
[3,5]	2 (1*2)	3	[5]
[5]	6 (2*3)	5	[]
[]	30 (6*5)	None	None

The last arriving Product, 30, will3 be handled by the clause for the empty list and reported as the return value for product/2. When product/1 receives that value, it will also report 30 as its return value and exit.

Because Erlang strings are lists of characters represented as numbers, you can do some strange things like enter `overall:product("funny")`. `product/1` will interpret the character values as numbers, and return `17472569400`.

Creating Lists with Heads and Tails

While there are times you want to calculate a single value from a list, most list processing involves modifying lists or converting a list into another list. Because you can't actually change a list, modifying or converting a list means creating a new list. To do that, you use the same vertical bar head/tail syntax, but on the right side of the pattern match instead of the left. You can try this out in the console, though it's more useful in a module:

```
1> X=[1|[2,3]].
[1,2,3]
```

Erlang interprets `[1|[2,3]]` as creating a list. If the value to the right of the vertical bar is a list, it gets appended to the head as a list. In this case, the result is a neat list of numbers. There are a few other forms you should be aware of:

```
2> Y=[1,2 | [3]].
[1,2,3]
3> Z=[1,2 | 3].
[1,2|3]
```

In line 2, there isn't a list wrapped around the now two items in the head, but the constructor still blends the head and the tail together seamlessly. (If you do wrap them in square brackets, the list constructor assumes that you want a list as the first item in the list, so `[[1,2] | [3]]` will produce `[[1,2],3]`.)

However, line 3 demonstrates what happens if you don't wrap the tail in square brackets—you get a list, called an *improper list*, that still contains a constructor, with a strange tail. Until you've learned your way quite thoroughly around Erlang, you should avoid this, as it will create runtime errors if you try to process it as a normal list. Eventually you may find reasons to do this, or encounter code that uses it.

More typically, you'll use list constructors to build lists inside of recursive functions. Example 6-2, which you can find in *ch06/ex2-drop*, starts from a set of tuples representing planemos and distances. With the help of the `drop` module from Example 3-8, it creates a list of velocities for the corresponding falls.

Example 6-2. Calculating a series of drop velocities, with an error

```
-module(listdrop).
-export([falls/1]).
```

```
falls(List) -> falls(List,[]).

falls([], Results) -> Results;
falls([Head|Tail], Results) -> falls(Tail, [drop:fall_velocity(Head) | Results]).
```

Much of this is familiar from Example 6-1, except that the Results variable gets a list instead of a number, and the last line of falls/2 creates a list instead of a single value. If you run it, however, you'll see one minor problem:

```
1> c(drop).
{ok,drop}
2> c(listdrop).
{ok,listdrop}
3> listdrop:falls([{earth,20},{moon,20},{mars,20}]).
[12.181953866272849,8.0,19.79898987322333]
```

The resulting velocities are reversed: the Earth has more gravity than Mars, and objects should fall faster on Earth. What happened? That last key line in falls/2 is reading a list from the beginning to the end, and creating a list from the end to the beginning. That puts the values in the wrong order. Fortunately, as Example 6-3 demonstrates, this is easy to fix. You need to call lists:reverse/1 in the clause of the falls/2 function that handles the empty list.

Example 6-3. Calculating a series of drop velocities, with the error fixed

```
-module(listdrop).
-export([falls/1]).

falls(List) -> falls(List,[]).

falls([], Results) -> lists:reverse(Results);
falls([Head|Tail], Results) -> falls(Tail, [drop:fall_velocity(Head) | Results]).
```

Now it works:

```
4> c(listdrop).
{ok,listdrop}
5> listdrop:falls([{earth,20},{moon,20},{mars,20}]).
[19.79898987322333,8.0,12.181953866272849]
```

 You could instead have put the lists:reverse/1 call in the falls/1 gateway function. Either way is fine, though I prefer to have falls/2 return a finished result.

Mixing Lists and Tuples

As you get deeper into Erlang and pass around more complex data structures, you may find that you're processing lists full of tuples, or that it would be more convenient to rearrange two lists into a single list of tuples or vice-versa. The lists module includes easy solutions to these kinds of transformations and searches.

The simplest set of tools are the lists:zip/2 and lists:unzip/1 functions. They can turn two lists of the same size into a list of tuples or a list of tuples into two lists.

```
1> List1=[1,2,4,8,16].
[1,2,4,8,16]
2> List2=[a,b,c,d,e].
[a,b,c,d,e]
3> TupleList=lists:zip(List1,List2).
[{1,a},{2,b},{4,c},{8,d},{16,e}]
4> SeparateLists=lists:unzip(TupleList).
{[1,2,4,8,16],[a,b,c,d,e]}
```

The two lists, List1 and List2, have different content, but the same number of items. The lists:zip/2 function returns a list containing a tuple for each of the items in the original list. The lists:unzip/1 function takes that list of two-component tuples and splits it out into a tuple containing two lists.

 Erlang also provides lists:zip3/3 and lists:unzip3/1, which do the same combining and separating on sets of three lists or tuple values.

You will also likely encounter times when you need to process a different kind of list containing tuples, a collection of values identified by keys. Many languages include associative arrays, where access is provided through key values, but Erlang's lists are always sequential, and have no built-in concept of retrieving information with a key. However, the lists module provides functions that support treating a list of tuples as if it were a key/value store, such as a hash table, hash tree, or associative array.

These days, more and more Erlang programmers are using maps, described in Chapter 10, for this kind of work. However, you may find old code that requires you to work with tuples inside lists. The key must be in a consistent location in the tuples stored in the list. Because the functions let you specify the location, you can put them anywhere in the tuple as long as you're consistent, but for this example, they'll be in the first position.

The first function to explore is `lists:keystore/4`. It takes a key value, a position, a list that is the previous state of the key/value store (defined in line 1 of the following code sample), and a tuple. If no tuple has that key value, then the new tuple simply gets added to the list, as shown in line 2 of the following code sample. If, as in line 3, a tuple already has that key value, the function will return a list that replaces the matched tuple with the new one:

```
1> Initial=[{1,tiger}, {3,bear}, {5,lion}].
[{1,tiger},{3,bear},{5,lion}]
2> Second=lists:keystore(7,1,Initial,{7,panther}).
[{1,tiger},{3,bear},{5,lion},{7,panther}]
3> Third=lists:keystore(7,1,Second,{7,leopard}).
[{1,tiger},{3,bear},{5,lion},{7,leopard}]
```

You can also pass `lists:keystore/4` an empty list for the array, and it will just return a list containing the new tuple.

Sometimes you want to replace a value *only* if it is present, not add a new value to the list. The similar `lists:keyreplace/4` will do just that.

```
4> Fourth=lists:keyreplace(6,1,Third,{6,chipmunk}).
[{1,tiger},{3,bear},{5,lion},{7,leopard}]
```

There was no item in the previous list with a key value of 6, so `lists:keyreplace/4` just returned a copy of the original list.

 All of these functions copy lists or create new modified versions of a list. As you'd expect in Erlang, the original list is untouched.

If you want to get information back out of a list, the `lists:keyfind/3` argument will report the data that matches a given key:

```
5> Animal5=lists:keyfind(5,1,Third).
{5,lion}
```

If the key isn't present, however, you'll just get a return value of `false`, instead of a tuple:

```
6> Animal6=lists:keyfind(6,1,Third).
false
```

Building a List of Lists

While simple recursion isn't too complicated, list processing has a way of turning into lists of lists in various stages. Pascal's triangle, a classic mathematical tool, is relatively simple to create but demonstrates more intricate work with lists. It starts with a 1 at the top, and then each new row is composed of the sum of the two numbers above it:

```
        1
      1   1
    1   2   1
  1   3   3   1
1   4   6   4   1
...
```

If those numbers seem familiar, it's probably because they're the binomial coefficents that appear when you put $(x+y)$ to a power. That's just the beginning of this mathematical marvel, described in more detail at *http://bit.ly/2lFAvGG*.

This is easily calculated with Erlang in a number of ways. You can apply the list techniques already discussed in this chapter by treating each row as a list, and the triangle as a list of lists. The code will be seeded with the first row—the top 1—represented as [0,1,0]. The extra zeros make the addition much simpler.

 This is not intended to be an efficient, elegant, or maximally compact implementation. At this point, a naive implementation likely explains more about lists. Once this makes sense, and you learn about list comprehensions in Chapter 7, you can explore what a vastly more compact version might look like. See *http://bit.ly/2loNXhFp*.

For a first step, Example 6-4 calculates rows individually. This is a simple recursive process, walking over the old list and adding its contents to create a new list.

Example 6-4. Calculating a row

```erlang
-module(pascal).
-export([add_row/1]).
add_row(Initial) -> add_row(Initial, 0, []).

add_row([], 0, Final) -> [0 | Final];

add_row([H | T], Last, New) -> add_row(T, H, [Last + H | New]).
```

The add_row/1 function sets things up, sending the current row a 0 to get the math started, and an empty list you can think of as "where the results go," though it is really an accumulator. The add_row/3 function has two clauses. The first checks to see if the list being added is empty. If it is, then it reports back the final row, adding a 0 at the front.

Most of the work gets done in the second clause of add_row/3. When it receives its arguments, the [H | T] pattern match splits the head of the list into the H value (a number) and the tail into T (a list, which may be empty if that was the last number). It also gets values for the Last number processed and the current New list being built.

It then makes a recursive call to add_row/3. In that new call, the tail of the old list, T, is the new list to process, the H value becomes the Last number processed, and the third argument, the list, opens with the actual addition being performed, which is then combined with the rest of the New list being built.

 Because the lists in the triangle are symmetrical, there is no need to use lists:reverse/1 to flip them. You can, of course, if you want to.

You can test this easily from the console, but remember that your test lists need to be wrapped in zeros:

```
1> c(pascal).
{ok,pascal}
2> pascal:add_row([0,1,0]).
[0,1,1,0]
3> pascal:add_row([0,1,1,0]).
[0,1,2,1,0]
4> pascal:add_row([0,1,2,1,0]).
[0,1,3,3,1,0]
```

Now that you can create a new row from an old one, you need to be able to create a set of rows from the top of the triangle, as shown in Example 6-5, which you can find in *ch06/ex4-pascal*. The add_row/3 function effectively counted down to the end of the list, but triangle/3 will need to count up to a given number of rows. The triangle/1 function sets things up, defining the initial row, setting the counter to 1 (because that initial row *is* the first row), and passing on the number of Rows to be created.

The triangle/3 function has two clauses. The first, the stop clause, halts the recursion when enough Rows have been created, and reverses the list. (The individual rows may be symmetrical, but the triangle itself is not.) The second clause does the actual work of generating new rows. It gets the Previous row generated from the list, and then it passes that to the add_row/1 function, which will return a new row. Then it calls itself with the new list, an incremented Count, and the Rows value the stop clause needs.

Example 6-5. Calculating the whole triangle with both functions

```
-module(pascal).
-export([triangle/1]).

triangle(Rows) -> triangle([[0,1,0]],1,Rows).

triangle(List, Count, Rows) when Count >= Rows -> lists:reverse(List);

triangle(List, Count, Rows) ->
  [Previous | _] = List,
  triangle([add_row(Previous) | List], Count+1, Rows).

add_row(Initial) -> add_row(Initial, 0, []).

add_row([], 0, Final) -> [0 | Final];

add_row([H | T], Last, New) -> add_row(T, H, [Last + H | New]).
```

Happily, this works.

```
5> c(pascal).
{ok,pascal}
6> pascal:triangle(4).
[[0,1,0],[0,1,1,0],[0,1,2,1,0],[0,1,3,3,1,0]]
7> pascal:triangle(6).
[[0,1,0],
 [0,1,1,0],
 [0,1,2,1,0],
 [0,1,3,3,1,0],
 [0,1,4,6,4,1,0],
 [0,1,5,10,10,5,1,0]]
```

Pascal's triangle may be a slightly neater set of lists than most you will process, but this kind of layered list processing is a very common tactic for processing and generating lists of data.

 You can learn more about working with lists in Chapter 2 of *Erlang Programming* (O'Reilly); Section 3.7 and Chapter 4 of *Programming Erlang*, 2nd Edition (Pragmatic); Section 2.2.5 of *Erlang and OTP in Action* (Manning); and Chapter 1 of *Learn You Some Erlang For Great Good!* (No Starch Press).

CHAPTER 7

Higher-Order Functions and List Comprehensions

Higher-order functions, functions that accept other functions as arguments, are a key place where Erlang's power really starts to shine. Unlike many languages, Erlang treats higher-order functions as a native and natural part of the language rather than an oddity. List comprehensions apply them in a compact style.

Simple Higher-Order Functions

Way back in Chapter 2, you saw how to use a fun to create a function:

```
1> Fall_velocity = fun(Distance) -> math:sqrt(2 * 9.8 * Distance) end.
#Fun<erl_eval.6.111823515>
2> Fall_velocity(20).
19.79898987322333
3> Fall_velocity(200).
62.609903369994115
```

Erlang not only lets you put functions into variables, it lets you pass functions as arguments. This means that you can create functions whose behavior you modify at the time you call it, in much more intricate ways than are normally possible with parameters. A very simple function that takes another function as an argument might look like Example 7-1, which you can find in *ch07/ex1-hof*.

Example 7-1. An extremely simple higher-order function

```
-module(hof).
-export([tripler/2]).

tripler(Value, Function) -> 3 * Function(Value).
```

The argument names are generic, but fit. `tripler/2` will take a value and a function as arguments. It runs the value through the function, and multiplies that result by three. In the shell, this might look like the following:

```
1> c(hof).
{ok,hof}
2> MyFunction=fun(Value)->20*Value end.
#Fun<erl_eval.6.111823515>
3> hof:tripler(6,MyFunction).
360
```

That defines another simple function taking one argument (and returning that number multiplied by 20), and stores it in the variable `MyFunction`. Then it calls the `hof:tripler/2` function with a value of six and the `MyFunction` function. In the `hof:tripler/2` function, it feeds the `Value` to the `Function`, getting back 120. Then it triples that, returning 360.

You can skip assigning the function to a variable if you want, and just include the `fun` declaration inside the `hof:tripler/2` function call:

```
4> hof:tripler(6,fun(Value)->20*Value end).
360
```

That may or may not be easier to read, depending on the functions and your expectations. This case is trivially simple, but demonstrates that it works.

 While this is a powerful technique, you can outsmart yourself with it easily. (I do!) Just as with normal code, you need to make sure the number and sometimes the type of your arguments line up. The extra flexibility and power can create new problems if you aren't careful.

`fun` has a few other tricks up its sleeve that you should know. You can use a `fun` to preserve context, even context that has since vanished:

```
5> X=20.
20
6> MyFunction2=fun(Value)->X * Value end.
#Fun<erl_eval.6.82930912>
7> f(X).
ok
8> X.
* 1: variable 'X' is unbound
9> hof:tripler(6,MyFunction2).
360
```

Line 5 assigns a variable named X a value, and line 6 uses that variable in a `fun`. Line 7 obliterates the X variable, as line 8 demonstrates, but line 9 shows that `MyFunction2` still remembers that X was 20. Even though the value of X has been flushed from the shell, the fun preserves the value and can act upon it. (This preservation is called a *closure*.)

You may also want to pass a function from a module, even a built-in module, to your (or any) higher-order function. That's simple, too:

```
7> hof:tripler(math:pi(), fun math:cos/1).
-3.0
```

In this case, the hof:tripler function receives the value pi and a fun, which is the math:cos/1 function from the built-in math module. Since the cosine of pi is -1, the tripler returns -3.0.

Creating New Lists with Higher-Order Functions

Lists are one of the best and easiest places to apply higher-order functions. Applying a function to all the components of a list to create a new list, sort a list, or break a list into smaller pieces is common. And you don't need to do much work to make it happen: Erlang's built-in lists module offers a variety of higher-order functions, listed in Appendix A, that take a function and list and do something with them. You can also use *list comprehensions* to do much of the same work. The lists module may seem easier at first, but as you'll see, list comprehensions are powerful and concise.

Reporting on a List

The simplest of these functions is foreach/2, which always returns the atom ok. That may sound strange, but foreach/2 is a function you'll call if and only if you want to do something to the list using side effects—like present the contents of a list to the console. To do that, define a simple function that applies io:format/2, here stored in the variable Print, and a List, and then pass them both to lists:foreach/2:

```
1> Print = fun(Value) -> io:format("  ~p~n",[Value]) end.
#Fun<erl_eval.6.111823515>
2> List = [1,2,4,8,16,32].
[1,2,4,8,16,32]
3> lists:foreach(Print,List).
  1
  2
  4
  8
  16
  32
ok
```

The lists:foreach/2 function walked through the list, in order, and called the function in Print with each item of the list as a Value. The io:format/2 function inside of Print presented the list item, slightly indented. When it reached the end of the list, lists:foreach/2 returned the value ok, which the console also displayed.

Most of the demonstrations in this chapter will be operating on that same List variable, containing [1,2,4,8,16,32].

Running List Values Through a Function

You might also want to create a new list based on what a function does with all of the values in the original list. You can square all of the values in a list by creating a function that returns the square of its argument, and passing that to lists:map/2. Instead of returning ok, it returns a new list reflecting the work of the function it was given:

```
4> Square = fun(Value)->Value*Value end.
#Fun<erl_eval.6.111823515>
5> lists:map(Square,List).
[1,4,16,64,256,1024]
```

There's another way to accomplish the same thing, with what Erlang calls *list comprehension*.

```
6> [Square(Value) || Value <- List].
[1,4,16,64,256,1024]
```

That produces the same resulting list, with different (and more flexible) syntax. While you saw the [A | B] syntax in list constructors, a list comprehension uses [A || B] syntax. That extra vertical bar changes the whole way this is interpreted. Instead of being a head and a tail, it's an expression—here a function—and a rule for extracting the arguments for that function from a list, called a *generator*.

In this case, the function is the fun you put in the Square variable on line 4. Its argument, Value, is taken on a walk through the List. That arrow (the <-) means "an element of," or if you want be more active, "comes from." You can read this list comprehension as "Create a list consisting of squares of a Value, where the Value comes from List."

Strictly speaking, the expression on the left doesn't have to be formally declared as a function. You can get the same results with something less formal:

```
7> [Value * Value || Value <- List].
[1,4,16,64,256,1024]
```

The multiplication operator (*) is technically a call to the */2 function, but any legal Erlang expression can be on the left of the ||.

Filtering List Values

The lists module offers a few different functions for filtering the content of a list based on a function you provide as a parameter. The most obvious, lists:filter/2, returns a list composed of the members of the original list for which the function returned true. For example, if you wanted to filter a list of integers down to values that could be represented as four binary digits, so numbers 0 or greater but less than 16, you could define a function and store it in Four_bits:

```
8> Four_bits = fun(Value)-> (Value<16) and (Value>=0) end.
#Fun<erl_eval.6.111823515>
```

Then, if you apply it to the previously defined List of [1,2,4,8,16,32], you'll get just the first four values:

```
9> lists:filter(Four_bits,List).
[1,2,4,8]
```

Once again, you can create the same effect with a list comprehension. This time, you don't actually need to create a function, but can instead use a guard-like construct (written *without* the when) on the right side of the comprehension:

```
10> [Value || Value <- List, Value<16, Value>=0].
[1,2,4,8]
```

If you also want a list of values that didn't match, lists:parti tion/2, shown in "Splitting Lists" on page 82, will return a tuple that contains the matched items in its first element and the unmatched items in its second.

Beyond List Comprehensions

List comprehensions are concise and powerful, but they lack a few key features available in other recursive processing. The only type of result they can return is a list, but there will be many times when you want to process a list and return something else, like a Boolean, a tuple, or a number. List comprehensions also lack support for accumulators, and don't let you suspend processing completely when certain conditions are met.

You could write your own recursive functions to process lists, but much of the time you'll find that the lists module already offers a function that takes a function you define and a list and returns what you need.

Testing Lists

Sometimes you just want to know if all the values—or any of the values—in a list meet specific criteria. Are they all of a specific type, or do they have a value that meets certain criteria?

The lists:all/2 and lists:any/2 functions let you test a list against rules you specify in a function. If your function returns true for all of the list values, both of these functions will return true. lists:any/2 will also return true if one or more values in the list results in your function returning true. Both will return false if your function consistently returns false.

 lists:all/2 and lists:any/2 don't necessarily evaluate the entire list; as soon as they hit a value that provides a definitive answer, they'll stop and return that answer.

```
11> IsInt = fun(Value) -> is_integer(Value) end.
#Fun<erl_eval.6.111823515>
12> lists:all(IsInt, List).
true
13> lists:any(IsInt, List).
true
14> Compare = fun(Value) -> Value > 10 end.
#Fun<erl_eval.6.111823515>
15> lists:any(Compare, List).
true
16> lists:all(Compare, List).
false
```

You can think of lists:all/2 as an and function applied to lists; more precisely like andalso because it stops processing as soon as it encounters a false result. Similarly, lists:any/2 is like or, or orelse, in this case stopping as soon as it finds a true result. As long as you need only to test individual values within lists, these two higher-order functions can save you from having to write a lot of recursive code.

Splitting Lists

Filtering lists is useful, but sometimes you want to know what didn't go through the filter, and sometimes you just want to separate items.

The lists:partition/2 function returns a tuple containing two lists. The first is the list items that met the conditions specified in the function you provided, while the second is the items that didn't. If the Compare variable is defined as shown in line 14 of the previous demonstration, returning true when a list value is greater than 10, then you can easily split a list into a list of items greater than 10 and a list of items fewer than 10:

```
17> lists:partition(Compare,List).
{[16,32],[1,2,4,8]}
```

Sometimes you'll want to split a list by starting from the beginning—the head—and stopping when a list value no longer meets a condition. The lists:takewhile/2 and lists:dropwhile/2 functions create a new list that contains the parts of an old list before or after encountering a boundary condition. These functions aren't filters, and to make that clear, the examples use a different list than the rest of the examples in this chapter:

```
18> Test=fun(Value) -> Value < 4 end.
#Fun<erl_eval.6.111823515>
19> lists:dropwhile(Test, [1,2,4,8,4,2,1]).
[4,8,4,2,1]
20> lists:takewhile(Test, [1,2,4,8,4,2,1]).
[1,2]
```

Both functions run through a list from head to tail and stop when they reach a value for which the function you provide as the first argument returns false. The lists:dropwhile/2 function returns what's left of the list, including the value that flunked the test. It does not, however, filter out later list entries that it might have dropped if they had appeared earlier in the list. The lists:takewhile/2 function returns what was already processed, *not* including the value that flunked the test.

Folding Lists

Adding an accumulator to list processing lets you turn lists into much more than other lists, and opens the door to much more sophisticated processing. Erlang's lists:foldl/3 and lists:foldr/3 functions let you specify a function, an initial value for an accumulator, and a list. Instead of the one-argument functions you've seen so far, you need to create a two-argument function, accepting the current value in the list traversal and the accumulator. The result of that function will become the new value of the accumulator.

Defining a function that works within the folding functions looks a little different, because of the two arguments:

```
21> Divide=fun(Value, Accumulator) -> Value / Accumulator end.
#Fun<erl_eval.6.111823515>
```

This function divides its first argument—to be the `Value` coming from the list—by its second, the `Accumulator` passed to it by the function doing the folding.

Folding has one other key twist. You can choose whether you want the function to traverse the list from head to tail, with `lists:foldl/3`, or from tail to head, with `lists:foldr/3`. `foldl` means "fold from left to right," and `foldr` means "fold from right to left." If order doesn't change the result, you should go with `lists:foldl/3`, as its implementation is tail-recursive and more efficient in most situations.

The `Divide` function is one of those cases that will produce very different results depending on the direction in which you process the list (and the initial accumulator value). In this case, folding also produces different results than you might expect in a simple division. Given the usual `List` of `[1,2,4,8,16,32]`, it seems like going from left to right will produce 1/2/4/8/16/32, and going from right to left will produce 32/16/8/4/2/1, at least if you use an initial accumulator of 1. The functions don't produce those results, however:

```
22> 1/2/4/8/16/32.
3.0517578125e-5
23> lists:foldl(Divide,1,List).
8.0
24> 32/16/8/4/2/1.
0.03125
25> lists:foldr(Divide,1,List).
0.125
```

This code seems too simple to have a bug, so what's going on? Table 7-1 walks through the calculations for `lists:foldl(Divide,1,List)`, and Table 7-2 walks through `lists:foldr(Divide,1,List)` step by step.

Table 7-1. Recursive division of a list forwards with foldl/3

Value from List	Accumulator	Result of Division
1	1	1
2	1 (1/1)	2
4	2 (2/1)	2
8	2 (4/2)	4
16	4 (8/2)	4
32	4	8

Table 7-2. Recursive division of a list backwards with foldr/3

Value from List	Accumulator	Result of Division
32	1	32
16	32 (32/1)	0.5
8	0.5 (32/16)	16
4	16 (8/0.5)	0.25
2	0.25 (4/16)	8
1	8	0.125

Moving through a list step-by-step produces very different values. In this case, the simple Divide function's behavior changes drastically above and below the value 1, and combining that with walking through a list item by item yields results that might not be precisely what you expected.

The result of the foldl is the same as 32/(16/(8/(4/(2/ (1/1))))), while the result of the foldr is the same as 1/(2/(4/(8/(16/(32/1))))). The parentheses in those expressions perform the same restructuring as the fold, and the concluding 1 in each is where the initial accumulator value fits in.

Folding is an incredibly powerful operation. This simple if slightly weird example just used a single value, a number, as an accumulator. If you use a tuple as the accumulator, you can store all kinds of information about a list as it passes by, and even perform multiple operations. You probably won't want to try to define the functions you use for that as one-liners, but the possibilities are endless.

You can learn more about working with higher-order functions in Chapter 9 of *Erlang Programming* (O'Reilly); Section 4.3 of *Programming Erlang*, 2nd Edition (Pragmatic); Section 2.7 of *Erlang and OTP in Action* (Manning); and Chapter 6 of *Learn You Some Erlang For Great Good!* (No Starch Press). List comprehensions are in Chapter 9 of *Erlang Programming* (O'Reilly); Section 4.5 of *Programming Erlang*, 2nd Edition (Pragmatic); Section 2.9 of *Erlang and OTP in Action* (Manning); and Chapter 1 of *Learn You Some Erlang For Great Good!* (No Starch Press).

CHAPTER 8

Playing with Processes

While Erlang is a functional language, Erlang programs are rarely structured around simple functions. Instead, Erlang's key organizational concept is the *process*, an independent component (built from functions) that sends and receives messages. Programs are deployed as sets of processes that communicate with each other. This approach makes it much easier to distribute work across multiple processors or computers, and also makes it possible to do things like upgrade programs in place without shutting down the whole system.

But taking advantage of those features means learning how to create (and end) processes, how to send messages among them, and how to apply the power of pattern matching to incoming messages.

The Shell Is a Process

You've been working within a single process throughout this book so far, the Erlang shell. None of the previous examples sent or received messages, of course, but the shell is an easy place to send and (for test purposes, at least) receive messages.

The first thing to explore is the *process identifier*, often called a *pid*. The easiest pid to get is your own. In the shell you can just run the self() function:

```
1> self().
<0.36.0>
```

<0.36.0> is the shell's representation of a *triple*, a set of three integers that provide the unique identifier for this process. (You will probably get a different set of numbers when you try it, though.) This group of numbers is guaranteed to be unique within this run of Erlang, but are not guaranteed to be the same in the future. Erlang uses pids internally, but while you can read them in the shell, you can't type pids directly into the shell or into functions. Erlang much prefers that you treat pids as abstrac-

tions, though if you really want to address a process by its pid number, you can use the pid/3 shell function to do so.

Every process gets its own pid, and those pids function like addresses for mailboxes. Your programs will send messages from one process to another by sending them to a pid. When that process has time to check its mailbox, it will be able to retrieve and process the messages there.

Erlang, however, will *never* report that a message send failed, even if the pid doesn't point to a real process. It also won't report that a message was ignored by a process. It's up to you to make sure your processes are assembled correctly.

 Pids can even identify processes running on multiple computers within a cluster. You'll need to do more work to set up a cluster, but when you get there you won't have to throw away code you wrote with pids and processes built on them.

The syntax for sending a message is pretty simple: a function or variable containing the pid, plus the send operator (!) and the message.

```
2> self() ! test1.
test1
3> Pid=self().
<0.36.0>
4> Pid ! test2.
test2
```

Line 2 sent a message to the shell containing the atom test1. Line 3 assigned the pid for the shell, retrieved with the self() function, to a variable named Pid, and then line 4 used that Pid variable to send a message containing the atom test2. (The ! always returns the message, which is why it appears right after the sends in lines 2 and 4.)

Where did those messages go? What happened to them? Right now, they're just waiting in the shell's mailbox, doing nothing.

There's a shell function—flush()—that you can use to see what's in the mailbox, though it also removes those messages from the mailbox. The first time you use it, you'll get a report of what's in the mailbox, but the second time, the messages are gone, already read:

```
5> flush().
Shell got test1
Shell got test2
ok
6> flush().
ok
```

The proper way to read the mailbox, which gives you a chance to do something with the messages, is the `receive...end` construct, which puts the message content into a variable and lets you process it. You can test this out in the shell. The first of the following tests just reports what the message was, whereas the second expects a number and doubles it:

```
7> self() ! test1.
test1
8> receive X -> X end.
test1
9> self() ! 23.
23
10> receive Y->2*Y end.
46
```

So far, so good. However, if you make a mistake—if there isn't a message waiting, or if you provide a pattern match that doesn't work—the shell will just sit there, hung. Actually, it's waiting for something to arrive in the mailbox, but you'll be stuck. The easiest way out of that is to hit Ctrl-G, and then type q. You'll have to restart Erlang.

Another way to hang the system, one that can become mysterious in more complicated contexts, happens if you try to reuse X and Y after they become bound variables. For example, you can do this without a problem:

```
1> self() ! test1.
test1
2> receive X -> X end.
test1
3> self() ! test1.
test1
4> receive X -> X end.
test1
```

But if you change the value that goes to X the next time, Erlang isn't happy and will just hang on you:

```
5> self() ! test2.
test2
6> receive X -> X end.
```

The first time around, X was unbound and able to accept any value. The second time, X was bound, but could still accept the same value, in this case `test1`. The last time, X was bound, and it couldn't accept a new value, `test2`, so it didn't, and the console got stuck.

Spawning Processes from Modules

While sending messages to the shell is an easy way to see what's happening, it's not especially useful. Processes at their heart are just functions, and you know how to build functions in modules. The receive...end statement is structured like a case...end statement, so it's easy to get started.

Example 8-1, which is in *ch08/ex1-simple*, shows a simple—excessively simple—module containing a function that reports messages it receives.

Example 8-1. An overly simple process definition

```
-module(bounce).
-export([report/0]).

report() ->
  receive
    X -> io:format("Received ~p~n",[X])
  end.
```

When the report/0 function receives a message, it will report that it received it. Setting this up as a process means compiling it and then using the spawn/3 function, which turns the function into a free-standing process. The arguments for spawn/3 are the module name, the function name, and a list of arguments for the function. Even if you don't have any arguments, you need to include an empty list in square brackets, and a single argument should be a one-item list. The spawn/3 function will return the Pid, which you should capture in a variable, here Pid:

```
1> c(bounce).
{ok,bounce}
2> Pid=spawn(bounce,report,[]).
<0.38.0>
3> is_process_alive(Pid).
true
```

You can test to see if your process is alive with the erlang:is_process_alive/1 function:

```
3> is_process_alive(Pid).
true
```

Once you have the process spawned, you can send a message to that pid, and it will report that it received it:

```
4> Pid ! 23.
Received 23
23
ok
```

However, there's one small problem. The report process exited—it went through the receive clause only once, and when it was done, was done. If you try to send it a message, the message will be returned, and nothing will report an error, but you also won't get any notification that the message was received because nothing is listening any longer:

```
5> Pid ! 23.
23
6> is_process_alive(Pid).
false
```

To create a process that keeps processing messages, you need to add a recursive call, as shown in the receive statement in Example 8-2, in *ch08/ex2-recursion*.

Example 8-2. A function that creates a stable process

```
-module(bounce).
-export([report/0]).

report() ->
  receive
    X -> io:format("Received ~p~n",[X]),
        report()
  end.
```

That extra call to report() means that after the function shows the message that arrived, it will run again, ready for the next message. If you recompile the bounce module and spawn it to a new Pid2 variable, you can send it multiple messages, as shown here:

```
5> c(bounce).
{ok,bounce}
6> Pid2=spawn(bounce,report,[]).
<0.47.0>
7> Pid2 ! 23.
Received 23
23
ok
8> Pid2 ! message.
Received message
message
```

You can also pass an accumulator from call to call if you want, for a simple example, to keep track of how many messages have been received by this process. Example 8-3 shows the addition of an argument; in this case, just an integer that gets incremented with each call. You can find it in *ch08/ex3-counter*.

Example 8-3. A function that adds a counter to its message reporting

```
-module(bounce).
-export([report/1]).

report(Count) ->
```

```
receive
    X -> io:format("Received #~p: ~p~n",[Count,X]),
        report(Count+1)
end.
```

The results are pretty predictable, but remember that you need to include an initial value in the arguments list in the spawn/3 call:

```
1> c(bounce).
{ok,bounce}
2> Pid2=spawn(bounce,report,[1]).
<0.38.0>
3> Pid2 ! test.
Received #1: test
test
ok
4> Pid2 ! test2.
Received #2: test2
test2
ok
5> Pid2 ! another.
Received #3: another
```

Whatever you do in your recursive call, keeping it simple (and preferably tail-recursive) is best, as these can get called many, many times in the life of a process.

 If you want to create impatient processes that stop after waiting a given amount of time for a message, you should investigate the after construct of the receive clause.

You can write this function in a slightly different way that may make what's happening clearer and easier to generalize. Example 8-4, in *ch08/ex4-state*, shows how to use the return value of the receive clause, here the Count plus one, to pass state from one iteration to the next.

Example 8-4. Using the return value of the receive clause as state for the next iteration

```
-module(bounce).
-export([report/1]).

report(Count) ->
  NewCount = receive
    X -> io:format("Received #~p: ~p~n",[Count,X]),
        Count + 1
  end,
  report(NewCount).
```

In this model, all (though just one here) of the receive clauses return a value that gets passed to the next iteration of the function. If you use this approach, you can think of the return value of the receive clause as the state to be preserved between function calls. That state can be much more intricate than a counter—it might be a tuple, for instance, that includes references to important resources or work in progress.

Lightweight Processes

If you've worked in other programming languages, you may be getting worried. Threads and process spawning are notoriously complex and often slow in other contexts, but Erlang expects applications to be a group of easily spawned processes? That run recursively?

Yes, absolutely. Erlang was written specifically to support that model, and its processes weigh less than its competitors. Erlang processes are designed to impose absolutely minimal overhead cost. The Erlang scheduler gets processes started and distributes processing time among them, and also splits them out across multiple processors.

It is certainly possible to write processes that perform badly and to structure applications so that they wait a long time before doing anything. But you don't have to worry about those problems happening just because you're using multiple processes.

Registering a Process

Much of the time, pids are all you need to find and contact a process. However, you will likely create some processes that need to be more findable. Erlang provides a process registration system that is extremely simple: you specify an atom and a pid, and then any process that wants to reach that registered process can just use the atom to find it. This makes it easier, for example, to add a new process to a system and have it connect with previously existing processes.

To register a process, use the register/2 built-in function. The first argument is an atom, effectively the name you're assigning the process, and the second argument is the pid of the process. Once you have it registered, you can send it messages, using the atom instead of a pid:

```
1> Pid1=spawn(bounce,report,[1]).
<0.33.0>
2> register(bounce,Pid1).
true
3> bounce ! hello.
Received #1: hello
hello
ok
```

```
4> bounce ! "Really?".
Received #2: "Really?"
"Really?"
ok
```

If you attempt to call a process that doesn't exist (or one that has crashed), you'll get a bad argument error:

```
6> zingo ! test.
** exception error: bad argument
    in operator  !/2
        called as zingo ! test
```

If you attempt to register a process to a name that is already in use, you'll also get an error, but if a process has exited (or crashed), the name is effectively no longer in use and you can re-register it.

You can also use whereis/1 to retrieve the pid for a registered process (or undefined, if there is no process registered with that atom), and unregister/1 to take a process out of the registration list without killing it:

```
5> GetBounce = whereis(bounce).
<0.33.0>
6> unregister(bounce).
true
7> TestBounce = whereis(bounce).
undefined
8> GetBounce ! "Still there?".
Received #3: "Still there?"
"Still there?"
ok
```

 If you want to see which processes are registered, you can use the regs() shell command.

If you've worked in other programming languages and learned the gospel of "no global variables," you may be wondering why Erlang permits a systemwide list of processes like this. Most of the first half of this book, after all, has been about isolating change and minimizing shared context.

If you think of registered processes as more like services than functions, however, it may make more sense. A registered process is effectively a service published to the entire system, something usable from multiple contexts. Used sparingly, registered processes create reliable entry points for your programs, something that can be very valuable as your code grows in size and complexity.

When Processes Break

Processes are fragile. If there's an error, the function stops and the process goes away. Example 8-5, in *ch08/ex5-division*, shows a report/0 function that can break if it gets input that isn't a number.

Example 8-5. A fragile function

```
-module(bounce).
-export([report/0]).

report() ->
  receive
    X -> io:format("Divided to ~p~n",[X/2]),
        report()
  end.
```

If you compile and run this (deliberately) error-inviting code, you'll find that it works well so long as you only send it numbers. Send anything else, and you'll see an ERROR REPORT in the shell, and no more responses from that pid. It died:

```
1> c(bounce).
{ok,bounce}
2>  Pid3=spawn(bounce,report,[]).
<0.38.0>
3> Pid3 ! 38.
Divided to 19.0
38
ok
4> Pid3 ! 27.56.
Divided to 13.78
27.56
ok
5> Pid3 ! seven.

=ERROR REPORT==== 24-Aug-2016::20:59:43 ===
Error in process <0.38.0> with exit value: {badarith,[{bounce,report,0,[{file,
"bounce.erl"},{line,6}]}]}

seven
6> Pid3 ! 14.
14
```

As you get deeper into Erlang's process model, you'll find that "let it crash" is not an unusual design decision in Erlang, though being able to tolerate such errors and continue requires some extra work. Chapter 9 will show you how to find and deal with errors of various kinds.

Processes Talking Amongst Themselves

Sending messages to Erlang processes is easy, but it's hard for them to report back responses if you don't leave information about where they can find you again. Sending a message without including the sender's pid is kind of like leaving a phone message without including your own number: it might trigger action, but the recipient might not get back to you.

To establish process-to-process communications without registering lots of processes, you need to include pids in the messages. Passing the pid requires adding an argument to the message. It's easy to get started with a test that calls back the shell. Example 8-6, in *ch08/ex6-talking*, builds on the drop module from Example 3-2, adding a drop/0 function that receives messages and removing the fall_velocity/2 function from the export.

Example 8-6. A process that sends a message back to the process that called it

```
-module(drop).
-export([drop/0]).

drop() ->
 receive
   {From, Planemo, Distance} ->
     From ! {Planemo, Distance, fall_velocity(Planemo, Distance)},
     drop()
 end.

fall_velocity(earth, Distance) when Distance >= 0  -> math:sqrt(2 * 9.8 * Distance);
fall_velocity(moon, Distance) when Distance >= 0 -> math:sqrt(2 * 1.6 * Distance);
fall_velocity(mars, Distance) when Distance >= 0 -> math:sqrt(2 * 3.71 * Distance).
```

To get started, it's easy to test this from the shell:

```
1> c(drop).
{ok,drop}
2> Pid1=spawn(drop,drop,[]).
<0.38.0>
3> Pid1 ! {self(), moon, 20}.
{<0.31.0>,moon,20}
4> flush().
Shell got {moon,20,8.0}
ok
```

Example 8-7, which you'll find in *ch08/ex7-talkingProcs*, shows a process that calls that process to demonstrate that this can work with more than just the shell.

Example 8-7. Calling a process from a process, and reporting the results

```
-module(mph_drop).
-export([mph_drop/0]).

mph_drop() ->
  Drop=spawn(drop,drop,[]),
  convert(Drop).

convert(Drop) ->
 receive
   {Planemo, Distance} ->
     Drop ! {self(), Planemo, Distance},
     convert(Drop);
   {Planemo, Distance, Velocity} ->
     MphVelocity = 2.23693629 * Velocity,
     io:format("On ~p, a fall of ~p meters yields a velocity of ~p mph.~n",
     [Planemo, Distance, MphVelocity]),
     convert(Drop)
 end.
```

The mph_drop/1 function spawns a drop:drop/0 process when it is first set up, using the same module you saw in Example 8-6, and stores the pid in Drop. Then it calls convert/1, which will also listen for messages recursively.

If you don't separate the initialization from the recursive listener, your code will work, but will spawn new drop:drop/0 processes every time it processes a message instead of using the same one repeatedly.

The receive clause relies on the call from the shell (or another process) including only two arguments, while the drop:drop/0 process sends back a result with three. When the receive clause gets a message with two arguments, it sends a message to Drop, identifying itself as the sender and passing on the arguments. When the Drop returns a message with the result, the receive clause reports on the result, converting the velocity to miles per hour. (Yes, it leaves the distance metric, but makes the velocity more intelligible to Americans.)

As your code grows more complex, you will likely want to use more explicit flags about the kind of information contained in a message, like atoms.

Running Example 8-7 from the shell looks like the following:

```
1> c(drop).
{ok,drop}
2> c(mph_drop).
{ok,mph_drop}
3> Pid1=spawn(mph_drop,mph_drop,[]).
<0.59.0>
4> Pid1 ! {earth,20}.
On earth, a fall of 20 meters yields a velocity of 44.289078952755766 mph.
{earth,20}
5> Pid1 ! {mars,20}.
On mars, a fall of 20 meters yields a velocity of 27.250254686571544 mph.
{mars,20}
```

This simple example might look like it behaves as a more complex version of a function call, but there is a critical difference. In the shell, with nothing else running, the result will come back quickly—so quickly that it reports before the shell puts up the message—but this was a series of asynchronous calls. Nothing held and waited specifically for a returned message.

The shell sent a message to Pid1, the process identifier for mph_drop:convert/1. That process sent a message to Drop, the process identifier for drop:drop/0, which mph_drop:mph_drop:0 set up when it was spawned. That process returned another message to mph_drop:convert/1, which reported to standard output, in this case the shell. Those messages passed and were processed rapidly. However, in a system with thousands or millions of messages in motion, those passages might have been separated by many messages, and come in later.

Watching Your Processes

Erlang provides a simple but powerful tool for keeping track of your processes and seeing what's happening. It's called Observer, and it offers a minimal GUI that lets you look into the current state of your processes and see what's happening. Depending on how you installed Erlang, you may be able to start it from a toolbar, but you can always start it from the shell:

```
6> observer:start().
ok
```

You'll see something like Figure 8-1 appear, presenting an overview of your Erlang system. To get to your processes, click the Processes tab and then the "Name or Initial function" label to sort the list by process name. You may need to scroll down a little to find drop:drop/0, but you'll see something similar to Figure 8-2.

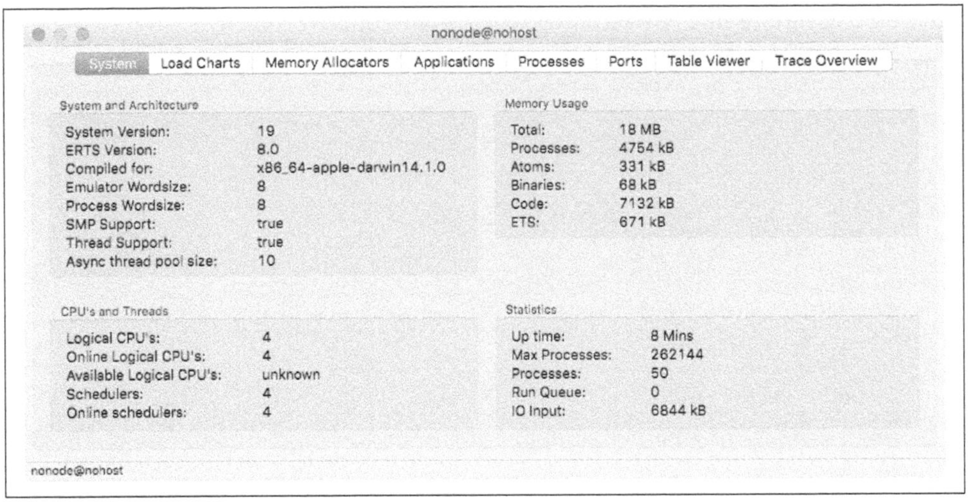

Figure 8-1. Observer at startup

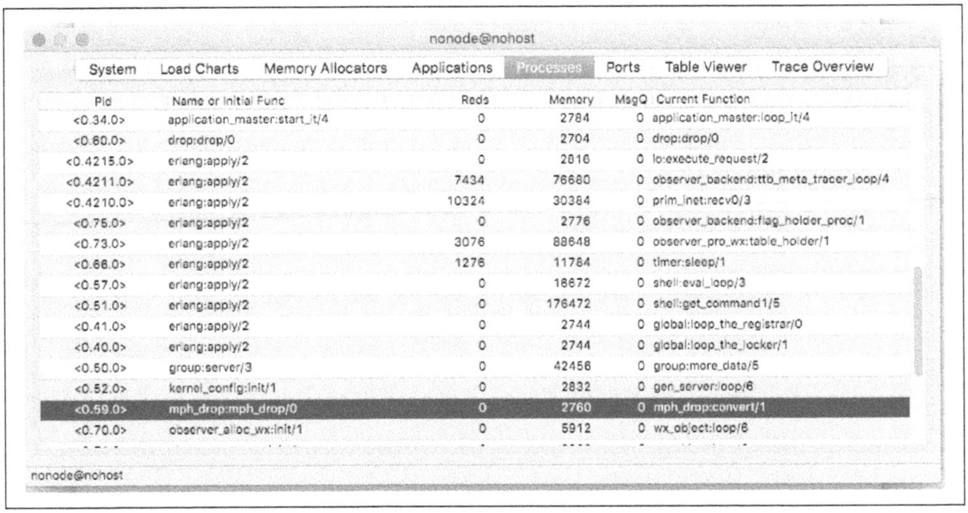

Figure 8-2. Observer's process window, sorted by process name

The list of processes is useful, but Observer also lets you look inside of process activity. If you double-click on a process, say `mph_drop:mph_drop/0`, you'll get some basic information about the process, as shown in Figure 8-3.

Figuring out what your process is doing, however, requires enabling tracing. First, find the `MphDrop:mph_drop/0` process in the list of processes, right-click it, choose "Trace selected processes by name (all nodes)," and select the options shown in Figure 8-4. Then click OK. You'll be back to the main window, where you should click the Trace Overview tab. Then click Start Trace. You will get a warning message, but you can ignore it. The Trace Log window will open, probably saying something like "Dropped Messages."

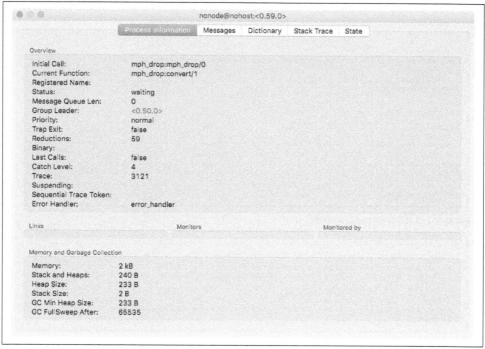

Figure 8-3. A closer look at mph_drop

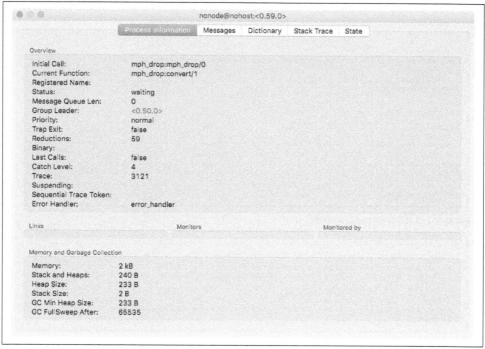

Figure 8-4. Basic trace options

Now you can see how messages flow.

```
7> Pid1 ! {earth,20}.
On earth, a fall of 20 meters yields a velocity of 44.289078952755766 mph.
{earth,20}
8> Pid1 ! {mars,20}.
```

```
On mars, a fall of 20 meters yields a velocity of 27.250254686571544 mph.
{mars,20}
```

The Observer Trace Log window for that process will update to show messages and calls, as shown in Figure 8-5. Just as in the normal Erlang syntax, ! means a message is sent. << means a message is received.

```
                                    Trace Log
*** Dropped 8 messages.
08:40:31:482364 (<0.59.0>) << {earth,20}
08:40:31:482445 (<0.59.0>) <0.60.0> ! {<0.59.0>,earth,20}
08:40:31:482506 (<0.59.0>) << {earth,20,19.79898987322333}
08:40:31:482566 (<0.59.0>) <0.50.0> ! {io_request,<0.59.0>,#Ref<0.0.1.5928>,
                                {put_chars,unicode,io_lib,format,
                                        ["On ~p, a fall of ~p meters yields a velocity
of ~p mph.~n",
                                        [earth,20,44.289078952755766]]}}
08:40:31:482729 (<0.59.0>) << {io_reply,#Ref<0.0.1.5928>,ok}
08:40:59:923718 (<0.59.0>) << {mars,20}
08:40:59:923795 (<0.59.0>) <0.60.0> ! {<0.59.0>,mars,20}
08:40:59:923845 (<0.59.0>) << {mars,20,12.181953866272849}
08:40:59:923915 (<0.59.0>) <0.50.0> ! {io_request,<0.59.0>,#Ref<0.0.1.5943>,
                                {put_chars,unicode,io_lib,format,
                                        ["On ~p, a fall of ~p meters yields a velocity
of ~p mph.~n",
                                        [mars,20,27.250254686571544]]}}
08:40:59:924073 (<0.59.0>) << {io_reply,#Ref<0.0.1.5943>,ok}
```

Figure 8-5. Tracing calls when you send mph_drop a message

The chain of messages starts with the call from the shell to <0.59.0>, with a tuple containing earth and 20. <0.59.0> sends that same tuple to <0.60.0>, which sends back the metric version of the velocity calculation. Because the trace is only following <0.59.0>, this gets reported with a << (a receive) with a tuple containing three values. Three values mean it's time to report. io:format turns out to send its own messages. A complex tuple starting with io_request brings the result back to the shell, and then the whole process repeats for the call about Mars.

Observer is generally the easiest place to turn when you're having difficulty figuring out what is happening among your processes.

Breaking Things and Linking Processes

When you send a message, you'll always get back the message as the return value. This doesn't mean that everything went well and the message was received and processed correctly, however. If you send a message that doesn't match a pattern at the receiving process, nothing will happen (for now at least); the message will land in the mailbox but not trigger activity. Sending a message that gets through the pattern matching but creates an error will halt the process where the error occurred, possibly even a few messages and processes down the line.

Messages that don't match a pattern in the `receive` clause don't vanish; they just linger in the mailbox without being processed. It is possible to update a process with a new version of the code that retrieves those messages.

Because processes are fragile, you often want your code to know when another process has failed. In this case, if bad inputs halt the `drop:drop/0`, it doesn't make much sense to leave the `mph_drop:convert/1` process hanging around. You can see how this works through the shell and Observer. First, start up Observer and spawn `mph_drop:mph_drop/0`.

```
1> observer:start().
ok
2> Pid1=spawn(mph_drop,mph_drop,[]).
<0.83.0>
```

If you switch to the Processes tab and click on the Pid header to sort them, you'll see something like Figure 8-6 in Observer. Then, feed your process some bad data, an atom (`zoids`) instead of a number for the `Distance`, and Observer will look more like Figure 8-7:

```
3> Pid1 ! {moon,zoids}.
{moon,zoids}
4>

=ERROR REPORT==== 19-Dec-2016::21:03:36 ===
Error in process <0.85.0> with exit value:
{badarith,[{drop,fall_velocity,2,[{file,"drop.erl"},{line,12}]},
          {drop,drop,0,[{file,"drop.erl"},{line,7}]}]}
```

Since the remaining `mph_drop:convert/1` process is now useless, it would be better for it to halt when `drop:drop/0` fails. Erlang lets you specify that dependency with a link. The easy way to do that while avoiding making your code race with itself is to use `spawn_link/3` instead of just `spawn/3`. This is shown in Example 8-8, which you can find in *ch08/ex8-linking*.

Example 8-8. Calling a linked process from a process so failures propagate

```
-module(mph_drop).
-export([mph_drop/0]).

mph_drop() ->
  Drop=spawn_link(drop,drop,[]),
  convert(Drop).

convert(Drop) ->
 receive
   {Planemo, Distance} ->
```

```
    Drop ! {self(), Planemo, Distance},
    convert(Drop);
  {Planemo, Distance, Velocity} ->
    MphVelocity= 2.23693629 * Velocity,
    io:format("On ~p, a fall of ~p meters yields a velocity of ~p mph.~n",
[Planemo, Distance, MphVelocity]),
    convert(Drop)
end.
```

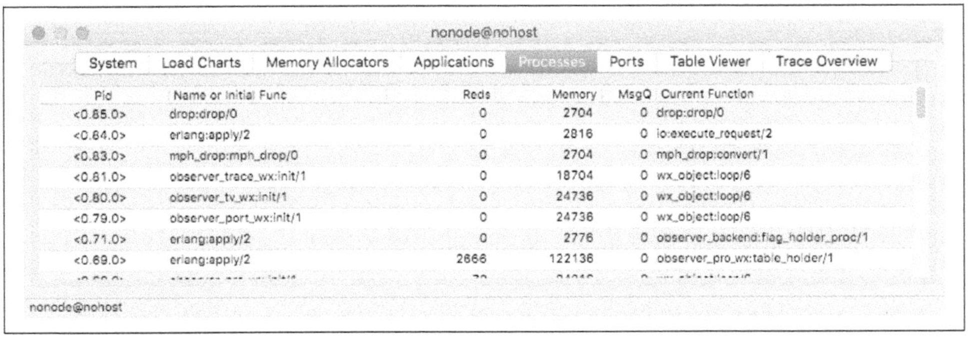

Figure 8-6. A healthy set of processes

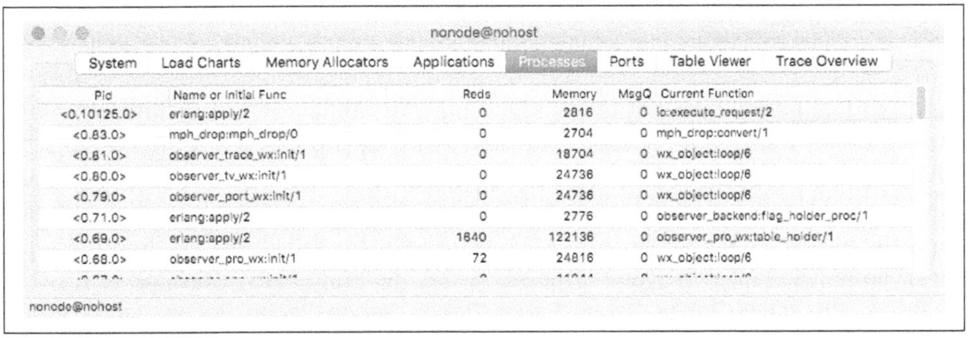

Figure 8-7. Only the drop:drop/0 process is gone

Now, if you recompile and test this out with Observer, you'll see that both processes vanish when drop:drop/0 fails, as shown in Figure 8-8:

```
1> c(drop).
{ok,drop}
2> c(mph_drop).
{ok,mph_drop}
3> observer:start().
ok
4> Pid1=spawn(mph_drop,mph_drop,[]).
<0.1004.0>
5> Pid1 ! {moon,zoids}.
{moon,zoids}
6>
```

```
=ERROR REPORT==== 19-Dec-2016::21:09:01 ===
Error in process <0.1005.0> with exit value:
{badarith,[{drop,fall_velocity,2,[{file,"drop.erl"},{line,12}]},
          {drop,drop,0,[{file,"drop.erl"},{line,7}]}]}
```

Pid	Name or Initial Func	Reds	Memory	MsgQ	Current Function
<0.2671.0>	erlang:apply/2	0	2816	0	io:execute_request/2
<0.91.0>	observer_trace_wx:init/1	0	15688	0	wx_object:loop/8
<0.90.0>	observer_tv_wx:init/1	0	24736	0	wx_object:loop/8
<0.89.0>	observer_port_wx:init/1	0	16832	0	wx_object:loop/8
<0.81.0>	erlang:apply/2	0	2776	0	observer_backend:flag_holder_proc/1
<0.79.0>	erlang:apply/2	1624	122136	0	observer_pro_wx:table_holder/1
<0.78.0>	observer_pro_wx:init/1	72	16960	0	wx_object:loop/8
<0.77.0>	observer_app_wx:init/1	0	11944	0	wx_object:loop/8
<0.76.0>	observer_alloc_wx:init/1	0	5912	0	wx_object:loop/8

nonode@nohost

Figure 8-8. Both processes now depart when there is an error

 Links are bidirectional. If you kill the the `mph_drop:mph_drop/0` process—with, for example, `exit(Pid1,kill)`.—the `drop:drop/1` process will also vanish. (`kill` is the harshest reason for an exit, and can't be stopped because sometimes you really need to halt a process.)

That kind of failure may not be what you have in mind when you think of linking processes. It's the default behavior for linked Erlang processes, and makes sense in many contexts, but you can also have a process trap exits. When an Erlang process fails, it sends an explanation to other processes that are linked to it in the form of a tuple. The tuple contains the atom EXIT, the Pid of the failed process, and the error as a complex tuple. If your process is set to trap exits, through a call to `process_flag(trap_exit, true)`, these error reports arrive as messages, rather than just killing your process.

Example 8-9, in *ch08/ex9-trapping*, shows how the initial `mph_drop/0` method changes to include this call to set the process flag, and adds another entry to the `receive` clause that will listen for exits and report them more neatly.

Example 8-9. Trapping a failure, reporting an error, and exiting

```
-module(mph_drop).
-export([mph_drop/0]).

mph_drop() ->
  process_flag(trap_exit, true),
  Drop=spawn_link(drop,drop,[]),
  convert(Drop).
```

```
convert(Drop) ->
 receive
   {Planemo, Distance} ->
     Drop ! {self(), Planemo, Distance},
     convert(Drop);
   {'EXIT', Pid, Reason} ->
     io:format("FAILURE: ~p died because of ~p.~n",[Pid, Reason]);
   {Planemo, Distance, Velocity} ->
     MphVelocity= 2.23693629 * Velocity,
     io:format("On ~p, a fall of ~p meters yields a velocity of ~p mph.~n",
[Planemo, Distance, MphVelocity]),
     convert(Drop)
 end.
```

If you run this code, and feed it bad data, the convert/1 method will report an error
message (mostly duplicating the shell) before exiting neatly.

```
1> c(mph_drop).
{ok,mph_drop}
2> Pid1=spawn(mph_drop,mph_drop,[]).
<0.45.0>
3> Pid1 ! {moon,20}.
On moon, a fall of 20 meters yields a velocity of 17.89549032 mph.
{moon,20}
4> Pid1 ! {moon,zoids}.
FAILURE: <0.46.0> died because of {badarith,
                                  [{drop,fall_velocity,2,
                                    [{file,"drop.erl"},{line,12}]},
                                   {drop,drop,0,
                                    [{file,"drop.erl"},{line,7}]}]}.

=ERROR REPORT==== 19-Dec-2016::21:13:46 ===
Error in process <0.46.0> with exit value: {badarith,[{drop,fall_velocity,2,
    [{file,"drop.erl"},{line,12}]},{drop,drop,0,[{file,"drop.erl"},{line,7}]}]}

{moon,zoids}
```

A more robust alternative would set up a new Drop variable, spawning a new process.
That version, shown in Example 8-10, which you can find at *ch08/ex10-resilient,* is
much tougher. Its receive clause sweeps away failure, soldiering on with a new copy
(NewDrop) of the drop calculator if needed.

Example 8-10. Trapping a failure, reporting an error, and setting up a new process

```
-module(mph_drop).
-export([mph_drop/0]).

mph_drop() ->
  process_flag(trap_exit, true),
  Drop=spawn_link(drop,drop,[]),
```

```
    convert(Drop).

convert(Drop) ->
  receive
    {Planemo, Distance} ->
      Drop ! {self(), Planemo, Distance},
      convert(Drop);
    {'EXIT', _Pid, _Reason} ->
      NewDrop=spawn_link(drop,drop,[]),
      convert(NewDrop);
    {Planemo, Distance, Velocity} ->
      MphVelocity= 2.23693629 * Velocity,
      io:format("On ~p, a fall of ~p meters yields a velocity of ~p mph.~n",
  [Planemo, Distance, MphVelocity]),
      convert(Drop)
  end.
```

If you compile and run Example 8-10, you'll see something like Figure 8-9 when you start Observer, go to Processes, and sort by Pid. If you feed it bad data, as shown on line 6 in the following code sample, you'll still get the error message from the shell, but the process will work just fine. As Observer shows in Figure 8-10, it started up a new process to handle the drop:drop/0 calculations, and as line 8 shows, it works like its predecessor:

```
1> c(drop).
{ok,drop}
2> c(mph_drop).
{ok,mph_drop}
3> observer:start().
ok
4> Pid1=spawn(mph_drop,mph_drop,[]).
<0.4294.0>
5> Pid1 ! {moon,20}.
On moon, a fall of 20 meters yields a velocity of 17.89549032 mph.
{moon,20}
6> Pid1 ! {mars,20}.
On mars, a fall of 20 meters yields a velocity of 27.250254686571544 mph.
{mars,20}
7> Pid1 ! {mars,zoids}.
{mars,zoids}
8>
=ERROR REPORT==== 19-Dec-2016::21:18:38 ===
Error in process <0.4295.0> with exit value:
{badarith,[{drop,fall_velocity,2,[{file,"drop.erl"},{line,13}]},
          {drop,drop,0,[{file,"drop.erl"},{line,7}]}]}
Pid1 ! {moon,20}.
On moon, a fall of 20 meters yields a velocity of 17.89549032 mph.
{moon,20}
```

Pid	Name or Initial Func	Reds	Memory	MsgQ	Current Function
<0.4296.0>	erlang:apply/2	0	2816	0	io:execute_request/2
<0.4295.0>	drop:drop/0	0	2744	0	drop:drop/0
<0.4294.0>	mph_drop:mph_drop/0	0	2744	0	mph_drop:convert/1
<0.91.0>	observer_trace_wx:init/1	0	68072	0	wx_object:loop/6
<0.90.0>	observer_tv_wx:init/1	0	16832	0	wx_object:loop/6
<0.89.0>	observer_port_wx:init/1	0	16856	0	wx_object:loop/6
<0.81.0>	erlang:apply/2	0	2776	0	observer_backend:flag_holder_proc/1
<0.79.0>	erlang:apply/2	3052	88648	0	observer_pro_wx:table_holder/1
<0.78.0>	observer_pro_wx:init/1	72	24816	0	wx_object:loop/6

nonode@nohost

Figure 8-9. Processes before an error (note the Pid for drop:drop/0)

Pid	Name or Initial Func	Reds	Memory	MsgQ	Current Function
<0.5382.0>	erlang:apply/2	0	2816	0	io:execute_request/2
<0.5381.0>	drop:drop/0	0	2744	0	drop:drop/0
<0.4294.0>	mph_drop:mph_drop/0	0	2744	0	mph_drop:convert/1
<0.91.0>	observer_trace_wx:init/1	0	68072	0	wx_object:loop/6
<0.90.0>	observer_tv_wx:init/1	0	16832	0	wx_object:loop/6
<0.89.0>	observer_port_wx:init/1	0	16856	0	wx_object:loop/6
<0.81.0>	erlang:apply/2	0	2776	0	observer_backend:flag_holder_proc/1
<0.79.0>	erlang:apply/2	4201	142832	0	observer_pro_wx:table_holder/1
<0.78.0>	observer_pro_wx:init/1	72	24816	0	wx_object:loop/6

nonode@nohost

Figure 8-10. Processes after an error (note the change in Pid for drop:drop/0)

Erlang offers many more process management options. You can remove a link with unlink/1, or establish a connection for just watching a process with erlang:moni tor/2. If you want to terminate a process, you can use exit/1 within that process, or exit/2 to specify a process and reason from another process.

Building applications that can tolerate failure and restore their functionality is at the core of robust Erlang programming. Developing in that style is probably a larger leap for most programmers than Erlang's shift to functional programming, but it's where the true power of Erlang becomes obvious.

You can learn more about working with simple processes in Chapter 4 of *Erlang Programming* (O'Reilly); Chapter 12 of *Programming Erlang*, 2nd Edition (Pragmatic); Section 2.13 of *Erlang and OTP in Action* (Manning); and Chapters 10 and 11 of *Learn You Some Erlang For Great Good!* (No Starch Press).

CHAPTER 9

Exceptions, Errors, and Debugging

"Let it crash" is a brilliant insight, but one whose application you probably want to control. While it's possible to write code that constantly breaks and recovers, it can be easier to write and maintain code that explicitly handles failure where it happens. Erlang is built to deal with problems like network errors, but you don't want to add your own mistakes to the challenges. However you choose to deal with errors, you'll definitely want to be able to track them down in your application.

Flavors of Errors

As you've already seen, some kinds of errors will keep Erlang from compiling your code, and the compiler will also give you warnings about potential issues, like variables that are declared but never used. Two other kinds of errors are common: runtime errors, which turn up when code is operating and can actually halt a function or process, and logic errors, which may not kill your program but can cause deeper headaches.

Logic errors are often the trickiest to diagnose, requiring careful thought and perhaps some time with the debugger, log files, or a test suite. Simple mathematical errors can take a lot of work to untangle. Sometimes issues are related to timing, when the sequence of operations isn't what you expect. In severe cases, race conditions can create deadlocks and halting; more mild cases can produce bad results and confusion.

Runtime errors can also be annoying, but they are much more manageable. In some ways you can view handling runtime errors as part of the logic of your program, though you don't want to get carried away. In Erlang, unlike many other environments, handling errors as errors may offer only minor advantages over letting an error kill a process and then dealing with the problem at the process level, as Example 8-10 showed.

Catching Runtime Errors as They Happen

If you want to catch runtime errors close to where they took place, the try…catch construct lets you wrap suspect code and handle problems (if any) that code creates. It makes it clear to both the compiler and the programmer that something unusual is happening, and lets you deal with any unfortunate consequences of that work.

For a simple example, look back to Example 3-1, which calculated fall velocity without considering the possibility that it would be handed a negative distance. The math:sqrt/1 function will produce a badarith error if it has a negative argument. Example 4-2 kept that problem from occurring by applying guards, but if you want to do more than block, you can take a more direct approach with try and catch, as shown in Example 9-1. (You can find it in *ch09/ex1-tryCatch*.)

Example 9-1. Using try and catch to handle a possible error

```
-module(drop).
-export([fall_velocity/2]).

fall_velocity(Planemo, Distance) ->
Gravity = case Planemo of
      earth -> 9.8;
      moon -> 1.6;
      mars -> 3.71
  end,

try math:sqrt(2 * Gravity * Distance) of
      Result -> Result
catch
      error:Error -> {error, Error}
end.
```

The calculation itself is now wrapped in a try. If the calculation succeeds, the pattern match following the of will be used. In this case, the calculation just produces one value, so matching the variable Result will put that value in Result, which then becomes the return value.

You can leave out the of clause entirely if you're only creating one value; the result of the expression in the try will become the returned value. You probably won't see of very frequently in code. This try…catch construct produces exactly the same results as in Example 9-1:

```
    try math:sqrt(2 * Gravity * Distance)
    catch
       error:Error -> {error, Error}
    end.
```

If the calculation fails, in this case because of a negative argument, the pattern match in the catch clause comes into play. In this case, the atom error will match the class or exception type of the error (which can be error, throw, or exit), and the variable Error will collect the details of the error. It then returns a tuple, opening with the atom error and the contents of the Error variable, which will explain the type of error.

You can try the following on the command line:

```
1> c(drop).
{ok,drop}
2> drop:fall_velocity(earth,20).
19.79898987322333
3> drop:fall_velocity(earth,-20).
{error,badarith}
```

When the calculation is successful, you'll just get the result. When it fails, the tuple tells you the kind of error that caused the problem. It's not a complete solution, but it's a foundation on which you can build.

You can have multiple statements in the try (much as you can in a case), separated by commas as usual. At least when you're getting started, it's easiest to keep the code you are trying simple so you can see where failures happened. However, if you wanted to watch for requests that provided an atom that didn't match the planemos in the case, you could put it all into the try:

```
fall_velocity(Planemo, Distance) ->
  try
      Gravity = case Planemo of
        earth -> 9.8;
        moon -> 1.6;
        mars -> 3.71
      end,
      math:sqrt(2 * Gravity * Distance)
  of
      Result -> Result
  catch
      error:Error -> {error, Error}
  end.
```

If you try an unsupported planemo, you'll now see the code catch the problem, at least once you recompile the code to use the new version:

```
4> drop:fall_velocity(jupiter,20).
** exception error: no case clause matching jupiter
      in function  drop:fall_velocity/2 (drop.erl, line 5)
5> c(drop).
{ok,drop}
6> drop:fall_velocity(jupiter,20).
{error,{case_clause,jupiter}}
```

The `case_clause` error indicates that a `case` failed to match, and the second component of that tuple, `jupiter`, tells you the item that didn't match.

You can also have multiple pattern matches in the `catch`. If your patterns don't match the error in the `catch` clause, it gets sent up through the stack, to see if something else catches it. If nothing does, it is reported as a runtime error, as if the `try` hadn't wrapped it.

If the code that might fail can create a mess, you may want to include an `after` clause after the `catch` clause and before the closing `end`. The code in an `after` clause is guaranteed to run whether the attempted code succeeds or fails, and can be a good place to address any side effects of the code. It doesn't affect the return value of the clause.

 Erlang also includes an older `catch` construct that doesn't use `try`. You may find this in someone else's code, but probably shouldn't include it in any new code that you write. It is less sophisticated and less readable than `try…catch`, though Chapter 11 shows one use for it in the shell.

Raising Exceptions with throw

You may want to create your own errors, or at least report results in a way that the `try…catch` mechanism can work with. The `throw/1` function lets you create exceptions that can then be caught (or left to kill a process, which might be reported to the shell). It often takes a tuple as an argument, letting you provide more detail about the exception, but you can use whatever you think is appropriate. But if you handle exceptions, you definitely want to handle exceptions close to where you want to raise them.

Using `throw/1` in the shell provides a simple example of what it does:

```
1> throw(my_exception).
** exception throw: my_exception
```

You can pattern match for thrown exceptions in a `catch` clause by using `throw` instead of `error`:

```
try some:function(argument)
  catch
    error:Error -> {found, Error};
    throw:Exception -> {caught, Exception}
  end;
```

You probably should save `throw` for cases where you can't come up with a better approach for signaling within your code, and be sure to use it only where you know you have nearby code that will catch it. Relying on other people and distant code to understand your invented exceptions may stretch their patience.

The preceding example used found and caught to distinguish between the different kinds of exceptions, but most code will likely just use error for both.

Logging Progress and Failure

The io:format/2 function is useful for simple communications with the shell, but as your programs grow (and especially as they become distributed processes), hurling text toward standard output is less likely to get you the information you need. Erlang offers a set of functions for more formal logging. They *can* hook into more sophisticated logging systems, but it's easy to get started with them as a way to structure messages from your application.

Three functions in the error_logger module give you three levels of reporting:

info_msg
> For logging ordinary news that doesn't require intervention.

warning_msg
> For news that's worse. Someone should do something eventually.

error_msg
> Something just plain broke, and needs to be looked at.

Like io:format, there are two versions of each function. The simpler version takes just a string, while the more sophisticated version takes a string and a list of arguments that get added to that string. Both use the same formatting structure as io:format, so you can pretty much replace any io:format calls you'd been using for debugging directly. All of these return ok.

As you can see, these calls produce reports that are visually distinctive, though warnings and errors get the same ERROR REPORT treatment:

```
1> error_logger:info_msg("The value is ~p. ~n",[360]).
ok

=INFO REPORT==== 12-Dec-2016::08:00:41 ===
The value is 360.
2> error_logger:warning_msg("Connection lost; will retry.").

=ERROR REPORT==== 12-Dec-2016::08:01:33 ===
Connection lost; will retry.
ok
Connection lost; will retry.ok
3> error_logger:error_msg("Unable to read database.~n").

=ERROR REPORT==== 12-Dec-2016::08:03:45 ===
```

```
Unable to read database.
ok
```

The more verbose form produces only a mild improvement over io:format, so why would you use it? Because Erlang has much much more lurking under the surface. By default, when Erlang starts up, it sets up the error_logger module to report to the shell. However, if you turn on SASL—the Erlang System Architecture Support Libraries, not the authentication layer—you'll be able to connect these notices to a much more sophisticated system for logging distributed processes. (If you just want to write your errors to disk, you should explore the error_logger:logfile/1 function.)

 It's possible to break the logger with bad format strings, so if you want more reliable logging, you may want to check into the more spartan _report versions of these functions.

While logging information is useful, it's not unusual to write code with subtle errors where you're not positive what to log where. You could litter the code with reporting, or you could switch to a different set of tools, Erlang's debugging facilities.

Debugging through a GUI

Erlang's graphical debugger is the friendliest place to start, requiring only a minor change in how you compile code to get started. This demonstration will use the same code shown in Example 9-1, but you need to compile it with the debug_info flag, and start the debugger with debugger:start(). You'll see a window like the one shown in Figure 9-1.

```
1> c(drop, [debug_info]).
{ok,drop}
2> debugger:start().
{ok,<0.71.0>}
```

When it first opens, the debugger window is pretty empty looking. You need to tell it what you want to watch, by choosing Interpret… from the Module menu. (Depending on your operating system, that may be a regular menu or look like a button in the top row). As shown in Figure 9-2, you should see the drop module (you may need to navigate to it if you didn't start in the same directory). If you select the drop module and click Choose, drop will appear in the left-hand pane of the Monitor window, as shown in Figure 9-3. You can then click Done to close the window and get back to the Monitor.

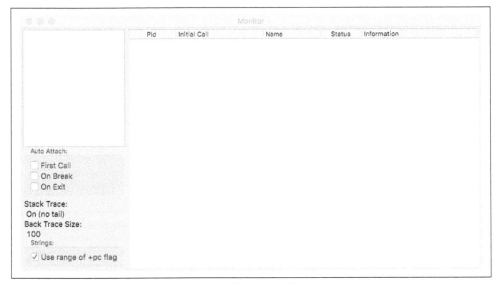

Figure 9-1. The debugger window when first opened

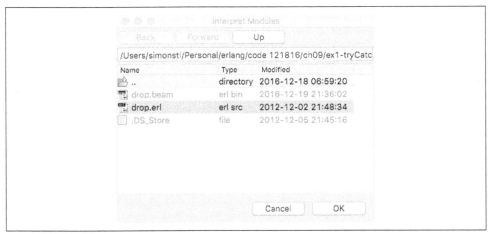

Figure 9-2. Choosing a module

The only way you'll know you actually selected the module is its appearance in the Monitor pane. If your windows are stacked and you can't see it, it's easy to think that nothing happened. But it did!

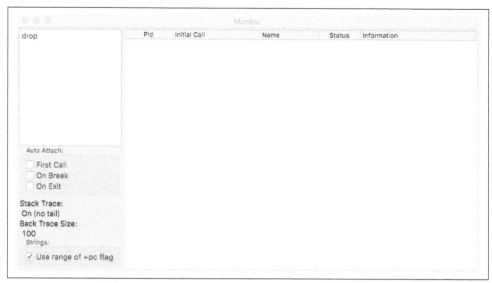

Figure 9-3. A module name appears on the left-hand side

Once the module name appears in the left-hand side of the Monitor window, the debugger is ready to watch it. You need to tell the debugger, however, what you want to see. If you double-click on the name of the module (drop), you'll get the View Module drop window shown in Figure 9-4, showing its code.

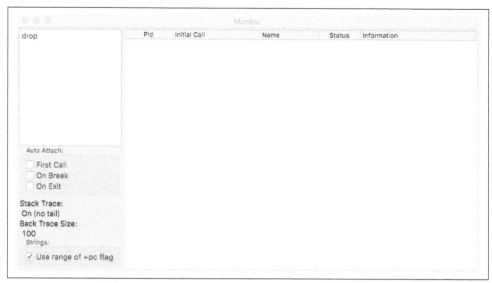

Figure 9-4. Examining the code for the drop module

You can add a breakpoint by clicking on a line of code, and then choosing Line Break… from the Break menu. You'll see the Line Break dialog shown in Figure 9-5, with reasonable default settings. Click OK, and the View Module drop window will change to indicate the breakpoint, as shown in Figure 9-6. You can close this window, and just leave the Monitor window open.

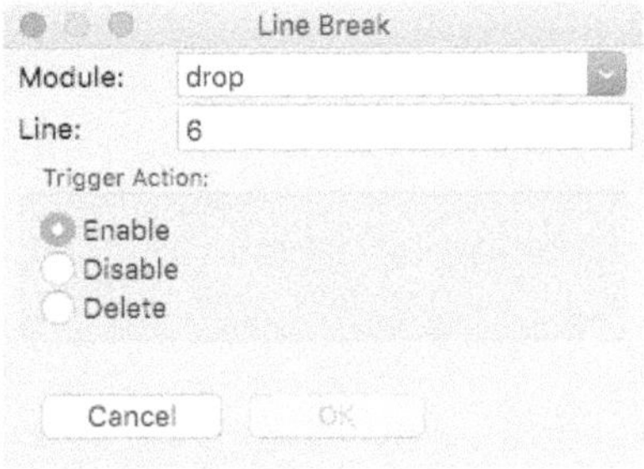

Figure 9-5. The Line Break dialog for setting breakpoints

Figure 9-6. The drop module with a breakpoint set on line 6

Now, if you go back to the shell and request:

```
3> drop:fall_velocity(earth,20).
```

You'll just get a pause. Nothing seems to happen, as the breakpoint stopped execution. However, in the Monitor window, you'll see a new entry in the table on the right-hand side, as shown in Figure 9-7. If you double-click that new entry, you'll get to the Attach Process window in Figure 9-8, which lets you step through the code line by line.

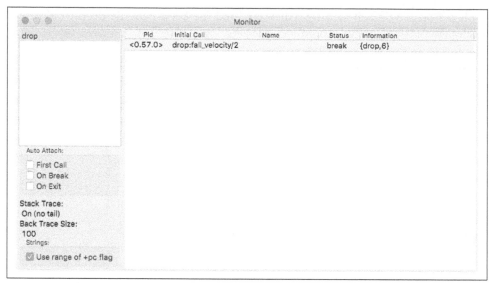

Figure 9-7. The Monitor window shows activity

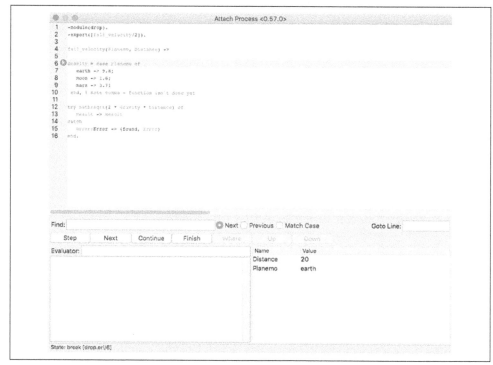

Figure 9-8. Code and bound values in the Attach Process window

Once you have the Attach Process window up, you can work through your code line by line (or tell it to continue) using the buttons in the middle line as follows:

Step

Execute the current line of code and move into the next line. If the next line of code to be executed is in another function (and that function is in a module compiled for debugging), you'll step through that function's code.

Next

Execute the current line of code and move to the next line of code in *this* module.

Continue

End the line-by-line stepping and just have the code execute as usual.

Finish

Similar to continue, but continues only for the current function. The debugger can keep working on the code when it returns from this function. (This is useful when you've stepped into a function whose details don't interest you and you don't have the patience to wait.)

Where

Moves the code window to the currently executing line.

Up and Down

Moves the code window up or down a function level in the stack.

Figures 9-9 through 9-12 show the results of stepping through the code executed by the drop:fall_velocity(earth,20) call. Note the changing bound variables and the final return to State: uninterpreted in Figure 9-12 when the call completes.

Any time the code is paused, you can use the Evaluator pane to make your own calculations using the values and functions available in the current scope. Unlike some debuggers, you can't change the value of the bound variables here—because you can't change the values of variables in Erlang generally.

In the end, the result also comes to the shell:

```
3> drop:fall_velocity(earth,20).
19.79898987322333
```

Figure 9-9. Stepping to the match on line 7

Figure 9-10. Next step: the try statement and calculation on line 12, with additional bound values

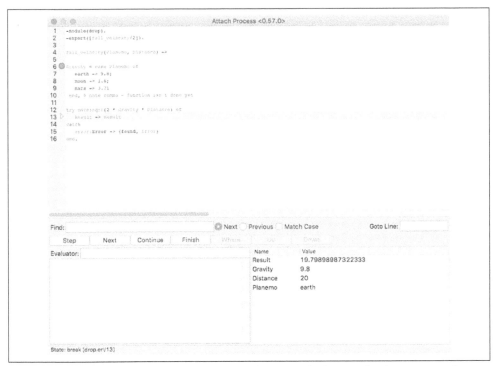

Figure 9-11. A successful calculation leads to line 13, which provides the return value

The debugger offers many more features, but this core set will get you started.

Tracing Messages

Erlang also offers a wide variety of tools for tracing code, both with other code (with the `trace` and `trace_pattern` built-in functions) and with a text-based debugger/reporter. The dbg module is the easiest place to start in this toolset, letting you specify what you want traced and showing you the results in the shell.

An easy place to get started is tracing messages sent between processes. You can use `dbg:p` to trace the messages sent between the `mph_drop` process defined in Example 8-8 and the `drop` process from Example 8-6. After compiling the modules—the `debug_info` flag isn't needed here—you call `dbg:tracer()` to start reporting trace information to the shell. Then you `spawn` the `mph_drop` process as usual, and pass that pid to the `dbg:p/2` process. The second argument here will be `m`, meaning that the trace should report the messages:

```
1> c(drop).
{ok,drop}
2> c(mph_drop).
{ok,mph_drop}
```

```
3> dbg:tracer().
{ok,<0.43.0>}
4> Pid1=spawn(mph_drop,mph_drop,[]).
<0.46.0>
5> dbg:p(Pid1,m).
{ok,[{matched,nonode@nohost,1}]}
```

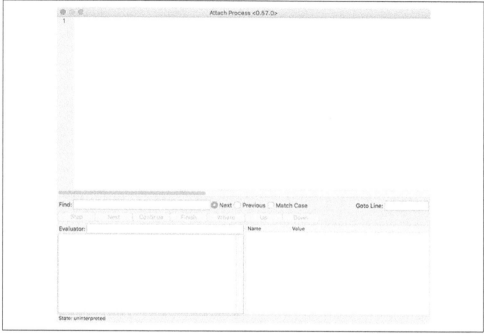

Figure 9-12. When the function call completes, the window goes mostly blank

 nonode@nohost just refers to the current Erlang environment when you aren't distributing processing across multiple systems. If you're running a distributed Erlang system, you'll have multiple nodes, each with its own independent Erlang runtime with its own name.

Now when you send a message to the mph_drop process, you'll get a set of reports on the resulting flow of messages. (<0.46.0> is the mph_drop process, and <0.47.0> is the drop process.)

```
6> Pid1 ! {moon,20}.
(<0.46.0>) << {moon,20}
(<0.46.0>) <0.47.0> ! {<0.46.0>,moon,20}
On moon, a fall of 20 meters yields a velocity of 17.89549032 mph.
(<0.46.0>) << {moon,20,8.0}
(<0.46.0>) <0.24.0> ! {io_request,<0.46.0>,<0.24.0>,
                        {put_chars,unicode,io_lib,format,
                            ["On ~p, a fall of ~p meters yields a
```

```
velocity of ~p mph.~n",
                                    [moon,20,17.89549032]]}}
{moon,20}
(<0.46.0>) << {io_reply,<0.24.0>,ok}
(<0.46.0>) << timeout
```

The << pointing to a pid indicates that that process received a message. Sends are indicated, as usual, with the pid followed by ! followed by the message. In this case:

- mph_drop (<0.46.0>) receives the message tuple {moon,20}.

- It sends a further message, the tuple {<0.46.0>,moon,20}, to the drop process at pid <0.47.0>.

- On this run, the report from mph_drop that "On moon, a fall of 20 meters yields a velocity of 17.89549032 mph." comes through faster than the tracing information. The rest of the trace indicates how that report got there.

- mph_drop receives a tuple {moon,20,8.0} (from drop).

- Then it calls io:format/2, which triggers another set of process messages to make the report, concluding with a timeout that doesn't do anything.

The trace reports come through a bit after the actual execution of the code, but they make the flow of messages clear. You'll want to learn to use dbg in its many variations to trace your code, and may eventually want to use match patterns and the trace functions themselves to create more elegant systems for watching specific code.

Watching Function Calls

If you just want to keep track of arguments moving between function calls, you can use the tracer to report on the sequence of calls. Chapter 4 demonstrated recursion and reported results along the way through io:format. There's another way to see that work, again using the dbg module.

Example 4-11, the upward factorial calculator, started with a call to fact:factorial/1, which then called fact:factorial/3 recursively. dbg will let you see the actual function calls and their arguments, mixed with the io:format reporting. (You can find it in *ch09/ex4-dbg*.)

Tracing functions is a little trickier than tracing messages because you can't just pass dbg:p/2 a pid. As shown on line 3 in the following code sample, you need to tell it you want it to report on all processes (all), and their calls (c). Once you've done that, you have to specify which calls you want it to report, using dbg:tpl as shown on line 4. It takes a module name (fact), function name (factorial), and optionally a match specification that lets you specify arguments more precisely. Variations on this function also let you specify arity.

So turn on the tracer, tell it you want to follow function calls, and specify a function (or functions, through multiple calls to dbg:tpl) to watch. Then call the function, and you'll see a list of the calls.

```
1> c(fact).
fact.erl:13: Warning: variable 'Current' is unused
fact.erl:13: Warning: variable 'N' is unused
{ok,fact}
2> dbg:tracer().
{ok,<0.38.0>}
3> dbg:p(all, c).
{ok,[{matched,nonode@nohost,26}]}
4> dbg:tpl(fact, factorial, []).
{ok,[{matched,nonode@nohost,2}]}
5> fact:factorial(4).
1 yields 1!
(<0.31.0>) call fact:factorial(4)
(<0.31.0>) call fact:factorial(1,4,1)
2 yields 2!
(<0.31.0>) call fact:factorial(2,4,1)
3 yields 6!
(<0.31.0>) call fact:factorial(3,4,2)
4 yields 24!
(<0.31.0>) call fact:factorial(4,4,6)
Finished.
(<0.31.0>) call fact:factorial(5,4,24)
24
```

You can see that the sequence is a bit messy here, with the trace reporting coming a little bit after the io:format results from the function being traced. Because the trace is running in a separate process (at pid <0.38.0>) from the function (at pid <0.31.0>), its reporting may not line up smoothly (or at all, though it usually does).

When you're done tracing, call dbg:stop/0 (if you might want to restart tracing with the same setup) or dbg:stop_clear/0 (if you know that when you start again you'll want to set things up again).

The dbg module and the erlang:trace functions on which it builds are incredibly powerful tools.

 You can learn more about error handling in Chapters 3 and 17 of *Erlang Programming* (O'Reilly); Chapter 6 of *Programming Erlang* (Pragmatic); Section 2.8 and Chapters 5 and 7 of *Erlang and OTP in Action* (Manning); and Chapters 7 and 12 of *Learn You Some Erlang For Great Good!* (No Starch Press).

CHAPTER 10

Storing Structured Data

Tuples and lists are powerful tools for creating complex data structures, but there are two key pieces missing from the story so far. First, tuples are relatively anonymous structures. Relying on a specific order and number of components in tuples can create major maintenance headaches. This also means that tuples don't let you refer to contents by name: you always have to know their location. Second, despite Erlang's general preference for avoiding side effects, storing and sharing data is a fundamental side effect needed for a wide variety of projects.

Four tools provide more support for structured data. Maps work well when you want to refer to possibly varied information through a single list of names. Records will help you create labeled orderly sets of information. Erlang term storage (ETS) will help you store and manipulate those sets, and the Mnesia database provides additional features for reliable distributed storage.

Mapping Your Data

Referring to data by its place in a list or tuple can tax programmer memory and code quickly, especially if data comes and goes. Erlang 17 (and later) addresses this common challenge with a new data structure, the map. Map processing is slightly slower than list or tuple processing, but is often easier to work with: you don't have to remember as much.

Creating a map requires a different syntax presenting keys and values:

```
1> Planemos = #{ earth => 9.8, moon => 1.6, mars => 3.71 }.
#{earth => 9.8,mars => 3.71,moon => 1.6}
```

The Planemos map now contains three items, with atoms as keys. The key earth references a value of 9.8, mars 3.71, and moon 1.6. The values are gravitational constants, though that doesn't need to be specified. Unlike records, coming up next, the different pieces don't get names.

The easiest way to extract values is with the Map module's `get` function:

```
2> maps:get(moon, Planemos).
1.6
```

If you need to add a value to a map, you can't—but you can ask for a new map that contains the values of the old map plus the new key-value pair, or a map that contains the old map minus a pair:

```
3> MorePlanemos = maps:put(venus, 8.9, Planemos).
#{earth => 9.8,mars => 3.71,moon => 1.6,venus => 8.9}
4> maps:get(venus, MorePlanemos).
8.9
5> FewerPlanemos = maps:remove(moon, MorePlanemos).
#{earth => 9.8,mars => 3.71,venus => 8.9}
```

Ask for a key that isn't there, and you'll get an error:

```
6> maps:get(moon, FewerPlanemos).
** exception error: {badkey,moon}
     in function  maps:get/2
        called as maps:get(moon,#{earth => 9.8,mars => 3.71,venus => 8.9})
```

While most of the power of maps remains locked in Map module functions and hasn't yet reached Erlang's own syntax, you can pattern match on maps:

```
17> #{earth := Gravity} = Planemos.
#{earth => 9.8,mars => 3.71,moon => 1.6}
18> Gravity.
9.8
```

If you need a flexible way to connect values with keys, maps may be what you're looking for. The Maps module also provides a variety of tools that support processing maps with higher-order functions. If you'd like more structure, you probably want to consider records.

 Maps appeared in Erlang 17, but are still slowly evolving and integrating into the language. Functions in the Maps module work, but only a few parts of the native Erlang syntax for maps have been implemented as of version 19. If you find examples online or even in books that don't work, they may be looking a little too far into the future.

From Tuples to Records

Tuples let you build complex data structures, but force you to rely on keeping the order and number of items consistent. If you change the sequence of items in a tuple, or if you want to add an item, you have to check through all of your code to make sure that the change propagates smoothly. As your projects grow, and especially if you need to share data structures with code you don't control, you'll need a safer way to store and address information.

Records let you create data structures that use names (rather than order) to connect with data. You can read, write, and pattern match data in a record without having to worry about the details of where in a tuple a field lurks or whether someone's added a new field.

 There are still tuples underneath records, and occasionally Erlang will expose them to you. Do not attempt to use the tuple representation directly, or you will add all the potential problems of using tuples to the slight extra syntax of using records.

Setting Up Records

Using records requires telling Erlang about them with a special declaration. It looks like a -module or -export declaration, but is a -record declaration:

```
-record(planemo, {name, gravity, diameter, distance_from_sun}).
```

That defines a record type named planemo, containing fields named name, gravity, diameter, and distance_from_sun. Right now, when you create a new record, the fields will all have the value undefined, but you can also specify default values if you prefer, for situations where there is a sensible normal option. For example, this declaration creates records for different towers for dropping objects:

```
-record(tower, {location, height=20, planemo=earth, name}).
```

Unlike -module or -export declarations, you'll often want to share record declarations across multiple modules and (for the examples in this chapter at least) even use them in the shell. To share record declarations reliably, just put the record declarations in their own file, ending with the extension *.hrl*. You can put each record declaration in a separate file or all of them in a single file, depending on your needs. To get started, and to see how these behave, you can put both of the declarations into a single file, *records.hrl*, as shown in Example 10-1. (You can find it in *ch10/ex1-records.*)

Example 10-1. A records.hrl file containing two rather unrelated record declarations

```
-record(planemo, {name, gravity, diameter, distance_from_sun}).
-record(tower, {location, height=20, planemo=earth, name}).
```

You may want to put individual record declarations into their own files and import them separately, bringing them in only when you actually need to get data into or out of a particular record type. This can be especially important if you're mixing code in cases where different developers used the same name for a record type but different underlying structures.

The command rr (for read records) lets you bring this into the shell:

```
1> rr("records.hrl").
[planemo,tower]
```

The shell now understands records with the names planemo and tower.

You can also declare records directly in the shell with the rd/2 function, but if you're doing anything more than just poking around, it's easier to have them in a formal imported declaration, which is a more reliable approach. You can call rl/0 if you want to see what records are defined, or rl/1 if you want to see how a specific record is defined.

Creating and Reading Records

You can now create variables that contain new records. The syntax for referencing records prefaces the name of the record type with a #, and encloses name-value pairs in curly brackets. For example, you could create towers with syntax like the following:

```
2> Tower1=#tower{}.
#tower{location = undefined,height = 20,planemo = earth,
       name = undefined}
3> Tower2=#tower{location="Grand Canyon"}.
#tower{location = "Grand Canyon",height = 20,
       planemo = earth,name = undefined}
4> Tower3=#tower{location="NYC", height=241, name="Woolworth Building"}.
#tower{location = "NYC",height = 241,planemo = earth,
       name = "Woolworth Building"}
5> Tower4=#tower{location="Rupes Altai 241", height=500, planemo=moon,
    name="Piccolomini View"}.
#tower{location = "Rupes Altai 241",height = 500,
       planemo = moon,name = "Piccolomini View"}
6> Tower5=#tower{planemo=mars, height=500, name="Daga Vallis",
    location="Valles Marineris"}.
#tower{location = "Valles Marineris",height = 500,
       planemo = mars,name = "Daga Vallis"}
```

These towers (or at least drop sites) demonstrate a variety of ways to use the record syntax to create variables as well as interactions with the default values:

- Line 2 just creates `Tower1` with the default values. You can add real values later.
- Line 3 creates a `Tower2` with a `location`, but otherwise relies on the default values.
- Line 4 overrides the default values for `location`, `height`, and `name`, but leaves the `planemo` alone.
- Line 5 replaces all of the default values with new values.
- Line 6 replaces all of the default values, and also demonstrates that *it doesn't matter in what order you list the name/value pairs.* Erlang will sort it out.

You can read record entries with two different approaches. To extract a single value, you can use a dot (.) syntax that may look familiar from other languages. For example, to find out which `planemo` `Tower5` is on, you could write:

```
7> Tower5#tower.planemo.
mars
```

You could also use pattern matching to extract several pieces simultaneously:

```
8> #tower{location=L5, height=H5} = Tower5.
#tower{location = "Valles Marineris",height = 500,
       planemo = mars,name = "Daga Vallis"}
9> L5.
"Valles Marineris"
10> H5.
500
```

The syntax feels a little backward, with the variable being bound on the right side of the equals sign instead of in its usual place on the left.

As always, you can't write a new value to an existing variable, but you can create a new record based on the values of an old one. The syntax used on line 12 is much like that used for assigning the contents of a field to a variable, but with a value in place of the variable name:

```
11> Tower5.
#tower{location = "Valles Marineris",height = 500,
       planemo = mars,name = "Daga Vallis"}
12> Tower5a=Tower5#tower{height=512}.
#tower{location = "Valles Marineris",height = 512,
       planemo = mars,name = "Daga Vallis"}
```

Yes, you always need to specify the record type. Yes, it's a bit of extra typing.

If you ever want to make the shell forget your record declarations, you can issue the shell command rf(). Your record-based variables will still exist, in a raw tuple form you should avoid ever using.

Using Records in Functions and Modules

Records also work well in modules using the same declaration files. You *can*, of course, just include the record declaration in every module that uses it, but that will require you to hunt down every declaration and update it if you ever want to change it. The saner approach is to use the files like the ones previously shown. You can do that easily with a single extra declaration near the top of your module:

```
-include("records.hrl").
```

Once you have the record declaration included, you can pattern match against records submitted as arguments. The simplest way to do this is to just match against the type of the record, as shown in Example 10-2, which is also in *ch10/ex1-records*.

Example 10-2. A method that pattern matches a complete record

```
-module(record_drop).
-export([fall_velocity/1]).
-include("records.hrl").

fall_velocity(#tower{} = T) ->
    fall_velocity(T#tower.planemo, T#tower.height).

fall_velocity(earth, Distance) when Distance >= 0  -> math:sqrt(2 * 9.8 * Distance);
fall_velocity(moon, Distance) when Distance >= 0 -> math:sqrt(2 * 1.6 * Distance);
fall_velocity(mars, Distance) when Distance >= 0 -> math:sqrt(2 * 3.71 * Distance).
```

This code uses a pattern match that will match only tower records, and puts the record into a variable T. Once again, the syntax may seem backward, with T being on the right of the equals sign instead of on the left, but it works. Then, like the original code way back in Example 3-8, it passes the individual arguments to fall_velocity/2 for calculations, this time using the record syntax.

Short variable names suddenly seem more attractive when you have to append the name of the record type on every use. In simple functions this can work, but in more complex functions short names may prove confusing, especially if you have two variables containing the same kind of record.

Because you used the same -record declaration in both the shell and the module, you can use the records you created to test the function.

```
14> c(record_drop).
{ok,record_drop}
15> record_drop:fall_velocity(Tower5).
60.909769331364245
16> record_drop:fall_velocity(Tower1).
19.79898987322333
```

The record_drop:fall_velocity/1 function shown in Example 10-3 pulls out the planemo and binds it to Planemo, and pulls out height and binds it to Distance. Then it returns the velocity of an object dropped from that Distance just like earlier examples throughout this book.

You can also extract the specific fields from the record in the pattern match, as shown in Example 10-3, which is in *ch10/ex2-records*.

Example 10-3. A method that pattern matches components of a record

```
-module(record_drop).
-export([fall_velocity/1]).
-include("records.hrl").

fall_velocity(#tower{planemo=Planemo, height=Distance}) ->
    fall_velocity(Planemo, Distance).

fall_velocity(earth, Distance) when Distance >= 0  -> math:sqrt(2 * 9.8 * Distance);
fall_velocity(moon, Distance) when Distance >= 0 -> math:sqrt(2 * 1.6 * Distance);
fall_velocity(mars, Distance) when Distance >= 0 -> math:sqrt(2 * 3.71 * Distance).
```

Again, the syntax may seem backwards, but it lets you extract the individual fields. You can take the records created and feed them into this function, and it will tell you the velocity resulting from a drop from the top of that tower to the bottom.

Finally, you can pattern match against both the fields and the records as a whole. Example 10-4, in *ch10/ex3-records*, demonstrates using this mixed approach to create a more detailed response than just the fall velocity.

Example 10-4. A method that pattern matches the whole record as well as components of a record

```
-module(record_drop).
-export([fall_velocity/1]).
-include("records.hrl").

fall_velocity(#tower{planemo=Planemo, height=Distance} = T) ->
io:format("From ~s's elevation of ~p meters on ~p, the object will reach ~p m/s
before crashing in ~s.~n",[T#tower.name, Distance, Planemo, fall_velocity(Planemo,
Distance), T#tower.location ]).

fall_velocity(earth, Distance) when Distance >= 0  -> math:sqrt(2 * 9.8 * Distance);
fall_velocity(moon, Distance) when Distance >= 0 -> math:sqrt(2 * 1.6 * Distance);
fall_velocity(mars, Distance) when Distance >= 0 -> math:sqrt(2 * 3.71 * Distance).
```

If you pass a tower record to record_drop:fall_velocity/1, it will match against the individual fields it needs to do the calculation, and match the whole record into T so that it can produce a more interesting if not necessarily grammatically correct report.

```
17> record_drop:fall_velocity(Tower5).
From Daga Vallis's elevation of 500 meters on mars, the object will reach
60.909769331364245 m/s before crashing in Valles Marineris.
ok
18> record_drop:fall_velocity(Tower3).
From Woolworth Building's elevation of 241 meters on earth, the object
will reach 68.72845116834803 m/s before crashing in NYC.
ok
```

record_drop:fall_velocity/1 uses the ~s control sequence for the io:format/2 call. It just includes the contents of the string, without surrounding quotes.

You can learn more about working with records in Chapter 7 of *Erlang Programming*; Section 3.9 of *Programming Erlang*; Section 2.11 of *Erlang and OTP in Action*; and Chapter 9 of *Learn You Some Erlang For Great Good!*.

Storing Records in Erlang Term Storage

ETS is a simple but powerful in-memory collection store. It holds tuples, and since records are tuples underneath, they're a natural fit. ETS and its disk-based cousin DETS provide a (perhaps too) simple solution for many data management problems. ETS is not exactly a database, but does similar work, and is useful by itself as well as underneath the Mnesia database you'll see in the next section.

Every entry in an ETS table is a tuple (or corresponding record), and one piece of the tuple is designated the key. ETS offers a few different structural choices depending on how you want to handle that key. ETS can hold four kinds of collections:

Sets (`set`)
> Can contain only one entry with a given key. This is the default.

Ordered sets (`ordered_set`)
> Same as a set, but also maintains a traversal order based on the keys. Great for anything you want to keep in alphabetic or numeric order.

Bags (`bag`)
> Lets you store more than one entry with a given key. However, if you have multiple entries that have identical values, they get combined into a single entry.

Duplicate bags (`duplicate_bag`)
> Not only lets you store more than one entry with a given key, but also lets you store multiple entries with identical values.

By default, ETS tables are sets, but you can specify one of the other options when you create a table. The examples in this chapter will be sets because they are simpler to figure out, but the same techniques apply to all four table varieties.

> There is no requirement in ETS that all of your entries look at all similar. When you're starting out, however, it's much simpler to use the same kind of record, or at least tuples with the same structure. You can also use any kind of value for the key, including complex tuple structures and lists, but again, it's best not to get too fancy at the beginning.

All of the examples in the following section will use the `planemo` record type defined in the previous section, and the data in Table 10-1.

Table 10-1. Planemos for gravitational exploration

Planemo	Gravity (m/s^2)	Diameter (km)	Distance from Sun (10^6 km)
mercury	3.7	4878	57.9
venus	8.9	12104	108.2
earth	9.8	12756	149.6
moon	1.6	3475	149.6
mars	3.7	6787	227.9
ceres	0.27	950	413.7
jupiter	23.1	142796	778.3
saturn	9.0	120660	1427.0

Planemo	Gravity (m/s²)	Diameter (km)	Distance from Sun (10⁶ km)
uranus	8.7	51118	2871.0
neptune	11.0	30200	4497.1
pluto	0.6	2300	5913.0
haumea	0.44	1150	6484.0
makemake	0.5	1500	6850.0
eris	0.8	2400	10210.0

Creating and Populating a Table

The `ets:new/2` function lets you create a table. The first argument is a name for the table, and the second argument is a list of options. There are lots and lots of options, including the identifiers for the table types just described, but the two most important for getting started are `named_table` and the tuple starting with `keypos`.

Every table has a name, but only some can be reached using that name. If you don't specify `named_table`, the name is there but visible only inside the database. You'll have to use the value returned by `ets:new/2` to reference the table. If you do specify `named_table`, processes can reach the table as long as they know the name, without needing access to that return value.

 Even with a named table, you still have some control over which processes can read and write the table through the `private`, `pro tected`, and `public` options.

The other important option, especially for ETS tables containing records, is the key pos tuple. By default, ETS treats the first value in a tuple as the key. The tuple representation underneath records (which you shouldn't really touch) always uses the first value in a tuple to identify the kind of record, so that approach works very badly as a key for records. Using the `keypos` tuple lets you specify which record value should be the key.

Remember, the record format for a `planemo` looks like the following:

```
-record(planemo, {name, gravity, diameter, distance_from_sun}).
```

Because this table is mostly used for calculations based on a given `planemo`, it makes sense to use the `name` as a key. An appropriate declaration for setting up the ETS table might look like the following:

```
PlanemoTable=ets:new(planemos,[ named_table, {keypos, #planemo.name} ])
```

This gives the table the name planemos and uses the named_table option to make that table visible to other processes that know the name. Because of the default access level of protected, this process can write to that table but other processes can only read it. It also tells ETS to use the name field as the key. Because it doesn't specify otherwise, the table will be treated as a set—each key maps to only one instance of a record, and ETS doesn't keep the list sorted by key.

Once you have the table set up, as shown in Example 10-5, you use the ets:info/1 function to check out its details. (You can find this in *ch10/ex4-ets*.)

Example 10-5. Setting up a simple ETS table and reporting on what's there

```
-module(planemo_storage).
-export([setup/0]).
-include("records.hrl").

setup() ->
 PlanemoTable=ets:new(planemos, [named_table, {keypos, #planemo.name}]),
 ets:info(PlanemoTable).
```

If you compile and run this code, you'll get a report of an empty ETS table with more properties than you probably want to know about at the moment:

```
1> c(planemo_storage).
{ok,planemo_storage}
2> planemo_storage:setup().
[{compressed,false},
 {memory,317},
 {owner,<0.316.0>},
 {heir,none},
 {name,planemos},
 {size,0},
 {node,nonode@nohost},
 {named_table,true},
 {type,set},
 {keypos,2},
 {protection,protected}]
```

Most of this is either more information than you need or unsurprising, but it is good to see the name (planemos), size (0—empty!), and keypos (not 1, the default, but 2, the location of the name in the tuple underneath the record). It is, as the defaults specify, set up as a protected set. (nonode@nohost just refers to the current Erlang environment when you aren't distributing processing across multiple systems. If you're running a distributed Erlang system, you'll have multiple nodes, each its own independent Erlang runtime with its own name.)

You can set up only one ETS table with the same name. If you call `planemo_stor age:setup/0` twice, you'll get an error:

```
3> planemo_storage:setup().
** exception error: bad argument
    in function  ets:new/2
        called as ets:new(planemos,[named_table,{keypos,2}])
        in call from planemo_storage:setup/0 (planemo_storage.erl, line 6)
```

To avoid this, at least in these early tests, you'll want to use the `f()` shell command to clear out any previous tables. If you think you're likely to call your initialization code repeatedly after you figure the basics out, you can also test the `ets:info/1` for `undefined` to make sure the table doesn't already exist, or put a `try...catch` construct around the `ets:new/2` call.

A more exciting ETS table, of course, will include content. The next step is to use `ets:insert/2` to add content to the table. The first argument is the table, referenced either by its name (if you set the `named_table` option), or by the variable that captured the return value of `ets:new/2`. In Example 10-6, which is in *ch10/ex5-ets*, the first call uses the name, to show that it works, and the rest use the variable. The second argument is a record representing one of the rows from Table 10-1.

Example 10-6. Populating a simple ETS table and reporting on what's there

```
-module(planemo_storage).
-export([setup/0]).
-include("records.hrl").

setup() ->
PlanemoTable=ets:new(planemos, [named_table, {keypos, #planemo.name}]),

ets:insert(planemos,
 #planemo{ name=mercury, gravity=3.7, diameter=4878, distance_from_sun=57.9 }),
ets:insert(PlanemoTable,
 #planemo{ name=venus, gravity=8.9, diameter=12104, distance_from_sun=108.2 }),
ets:insert(PlanemoTable,
 #planemo{ name=earth, gravity=9.8, diameter=12756, distance_from_sun=149.6 }),
ets:insert(PlanemoTable,
 #planemo{ name=moon, gravity=1.6, diameter=3475, distance_from_sun=149.6 }),
ets:insert(PlanemoTable,
 #planemo{ name=mars, gravity=3.7, diameter=6787, distance_from_sun=227.9 }),
ets:insert(PlanemoTable,
 #planemo{ name=ceres, gravity=0.27, diameter=950, distance_from_sun=413.7 }),
ets:insert(PlanemoTable,
 #planemo{ name=jupiter, gravity=23.1, diameter=142796, distance_from_sun=778.3 }),
ets:insert(PlanemoTable,
 #planemo{ name=saturn, gravity=9.0, diameter=120660, distance_from_sun=1427.0 }),
ets:insert(PlanemoTable,
 #planemo{ name=uranus, gravity=8.7, diameter=51118, distance_from_sun=2871.0 }),
```

```
ets:insert(PlanemoTable,
 #planemo{ name=neptune, gravity=11.0, diameter=30200, distance_from_sun=4497.1 }),
ets:insert(PlanemoTable,
 #planemo{ name=pluto, gravity=0.6, diameter=2300, distance_from_sun=5913.0 }),
ets:insert(PlanemoTable,
 #planemo{ name=haumea, gravity=0.44, diameter=1150, distance_from_sun=6484.0 }),
ets:insert(PlanemoTable,
 #planemo{ name=makemake, gravity=0.5, diameter=1500, distance_from_sun=6850.0 }),
ets:insert(PlanemoTable,
 #planemo{ name=eris, gravity=0.8, diameter=2400, distance_from_sun=10210.0 }),
ets:info(PlanemoTable).
```

Again, the last call is to `ets:info/1`, which now reports that the table has 14 items:

```
4> c(planemo_storage).
{ok,planemo_storage}
5> f().
ok
6> planemo_storage:setup().
[{compressed,false},
 {memory,541},
 {owner,<0.342.0>},
 {heir,none},
 {name,planemos},
 {size,14},
 {node,nonode@nohost},
 {named_table,true},
 {type,set},
 {keypos,2},
 {protection,protected}]
```

If you want to see what's in that table, you have a couple of options. The quick way to do it in the shell is to use the `ets:tab2list/1` function, which will return a list of records (or tuples, if you leave out the record import on line 7):

```
7> rr("records.hrl").
[planemo,tower]
8> ets:tab2list(planemos).
[#planemo{name = pluto,gravity = 0.6,diameter - 2300,
          distance_from_sun = 5913.0},
 #planemo{name = saturn,gravity = 9.0,diameter = 120660,
          distance_from_sun = 1427.0},
 #planemo{name = moon,gravity = 1.6,diameter = 3475,
          distance_from_sun = 149.6},
 #planemo{name = mercury,gravity = 3.7,diameter = 4878,
          distance_from_sun = 57.9},
 #planemo{name = earth,gravity = 9.8,diameter = 12756,
          distance_from_sun = 149.6},
 #planemo{name = neptune,gravity = 11.0,diameter = 30200,
          distance_from_sun = 4497.1},
 #planemo{name = makemake,gravity = 0.5,diameter = 1500,
          distance_from_sun = 6850.0},
 #planemo{name = uranus,gravity = 8.7,diameter = 51118,
```

```
                      distance_from_sun = 2871.0},
       #planemo{name = ceres,gravity = 0.27,diameter = 950,
                      distance_from_sun = 413.7},
       #planemo{name = venus,gravity = 8.9,diameter = 12104,
                      distance_from_sun = 108.2},
       #planemo{name = mars,gravity = 3.7,diameter = 6787,
                      distance_from_sun = 227.9},
       #planemo{name = eris,gravity = 0.8,diameter = 2400,
                      distance_from_sun = 10210.0},
       #planemo{name = jupiter,gravity = 23.1,diameter = 142796,
                      distance_from_sun = 778.3},
       #planemo{name = haumea,gravity = 0.44,diameter = 1150,
                      distance_from_sun = 6484.0}]
```

If you'd rather keep track of the table in a separate window, Erlang's table visualizer shows the same information in a slightly more readable form. You can start it from the shell with observer:start(), and then click on the Table Viewer tab. You'll see something like Figure 10-1. Double-click on the planemos table, and a more detailed report on its contents like the one shown in Figure 10-2 will appear.

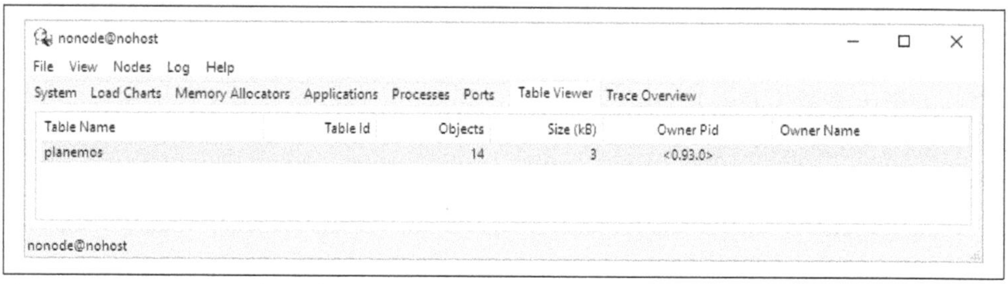

Figure 10-1. Opening the table visualizer

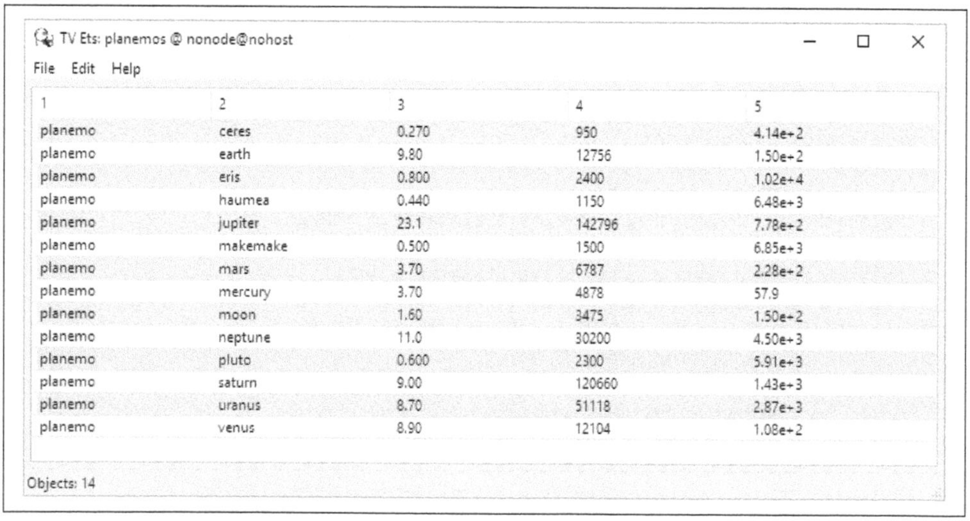

Figure 10-2. Reviewing the planemos table in the visualizer

The visualizer doesn't know about your record declarations.

> If you want to see a table of all the current ETS tables, try issuing ets:i() in the shell. You'll see the tables you've created (probably) near the bottom.

Simple Queries

The easiest way to look up records in your ETS table is with the ets:lookup/2 function and the key. You can test this easily from the shell:

```
9> ets:lookup(planemos,eris).
[#planemo{name = eris,gravity = 0.8,diameter = 2400,
         distance_from_sun = 10210.0}]
```

The return value is always a list. This is true despite Erlang knowing that this ETS table has the set type, so only one value can match the key, and despite there being only one value. In situations like this where you know that there will only be one returned value, the hd/1 function, which Example 5-5 showed for use with user inputs, can get you the head of a list quickly. Since there is only one item, the head is just that item.

```
10> hd(ets:lookup(planemos,eris)).
#planemo{name = eris,gravity = 0.8,diameter = 2400,
         distance_from_sun = 10210.0}
```

The square brackets are gone, which means you can now extract, say, the gravity of a planemo:

```
11> Result=hd(ets:lookup(planemos,eris)).
#planemo{name = eris,gravity = 0.8,diameter = 2400,
         distance_from_sun = 10210.0}
12> Result#planemo.gravity.
0.8
```

> You can also use pattern matching to extract the value instead of the hd/1 function, as in [Result]=ets:lookup(planemos,eris)..
> Both approaches will fail if the return value is an empty list.

A Key Feature: Overwriting Values

Up until now, you've had to work with (or around) Erlang's single-assignment paradigm: you can't overwrite the value of a variable, or change the value of an item in a list directly. However, ETS doesn't have that restriction. If you want to change the value of gravity on mercury, you can:

```
13> ets:insert(planemos, #planemo{ name=mercury,
  gravity=3.9, diameter=4878, distance_from_sun=57.9 }).
true
14> ets:lookup(planemos, mercury).
[#planemo{name = mercury,gravity = 3.9,diameter = 4878,
          distance_from_sun = 57.9}]
```

Just because you *can* change values in an ETS table, however, doesn't mean that you should rewrite your code to replace immutable variables with flexible ETS table contents. Nor should you make all your tables public so that various processes can read and write whatever they like to the ETS table, making it a different form of shared memory.

Try to remember the discipline you've had to learn up until this point. Ask yourself when making changes is going to be useful, and when it might introduce tricky bugs. You probably won't have to change the gravity of Mercury, but it certainly could make sense to change a shipping address. If you have doubts, lean toward caution.

ETS Tables and Processes

Now that you can extract gravitational constants for planemos, you can expand the drop module to calculate drops in many more locations. Example 10-7 combines the drop module from Example 8-6 with the ETS table built in Example 10-6 to create a more powerful drop calculator. (You can find this in *ch10/ex6-ets-calculator*.)

Example 10-7. Calculating drop velocities using an ETS table of planemo properties

```
-module(drop).
-export([drop/0]).
-include("records.hrl").

drop() ->
 setup(),
 handle_drops().

handle_drops() ->
 receive
  {From, Planemo, Distance} ->
  From ! {Planemo, Distance, fall_velocity(Planemo, Distance)},
  handle_drops()
 end.
```

```
fall_velocity(Planemo, Distance) when Distance >= 0 ->
  P=hd(ets:lookup(planemos,Planemo)),
  math:sqrt(2 * P#planemo.gravity * Distance).

setup() ->
 ets:new(planemos, [named_table, {keypos, #planemo.name}]),

 ets:insert(planemos,
  #planemo{ name=mercury, gravity=3.7, diameter=4878, distance_from_sun=57.9 }),
 ets:insert(planemos,
  #planemo{ name=venus, gravity=8.9, diameter=12104, distance_from_sun=108.2 }),
 ets:insert(planemos,
  #planemo{ name=earth, gravity=9.8, diameter=12756, distance_from_sun=149.6 }),
 ets:insert(planemos,
  #planemo{ name=moon, gravity=1.6, diameter=3475, distance_from_sun=149.6 }),
 ets:insert(planemos,
  #planemo{ name=mars, gravity=3.7, diameter=6787, distance_from_sun=227.9 }),
 ets:insert(planemos,
  #planemo{ name=ceres, gravity=0.27, diameter=950, distance_from_sun=413.7 }),
 ets:insert(planemos,
  #planemo{ name=jupiter, gravity=23.1, diameter=142796, distance_from_sun=778.3 }),
 ets:insert(planemos,
  #planemo{ name=saturn, gravity=9.0, diameter=120660, distance_from_sun=1427.0 }),
 ets:insert(planemos,
  #planemo{ name=uranus, gravity=8.7, diameter=51118, distance_from_sun=2871.0 }),
 ets:insert(planemos,
  #planemo{ name=neptune, gravity=11.0, diameter=30200, distance_from_sun=4497.1 }),
 ets:insert(planemos,
  #planemo{ name=pluto, gravity=0.6, diameter=2300, distance_from_sun=5913.0 }),
 ets:insert(planemos,
  #planemo{ name=haumea, gravity=0.44, diameter=1150, distance_from_sun=6484.0 }),
 ets:insert(planemos,
  #planemo{ name=makemake, gravity=0.5, diameter=1500, distance_from_sun=6850.0 }),
 ets:insert(planemos,
  #planemo{ name=eris, gravity=0.8, diameter=2400, distance_from_sun=10210.0 }).
```

The drop/0 function changes a little to call the initialization separately and avoid setting up the table on every call. This moves the message handling to a separate function, handle_drop/0. The fall_velocity/2 function also changes, as it now looks up planemo names in the ETS table and gets their gravitational constant from that table rather than hardcoding those contents into the function. (While it would certainly be possible to pass the PlanemoTable variable from the previous example as an argument to the recursive message handler, it's simpler to just use it as a named table.)

If this process crashes and needs to be restarted, restarting it will trigger the setup/0 function, which currently doesn't check to see whether the ETS table exists. That could cause an error, except that ETS tables vanish when the processes that created them die. ETS offers an heir option and an ets:give_away/3 function if you want to avoid that behavior, but for now it works well.

If you combine this module with the mph_drop module from Example 8-7, you'll be able to calculate drop velocities on all of these planemos:

```
1> c(drop).
{ok,drop}
2> c(mph_drop).
{ok,mph_drop}
3> Pid1=spawn(mph_drop,mph_drop,[]).
<0.33.0>
4> Pid1 ! {earth,20}.
On earth, a fall of 20 meters yields a velocity of 44.289078952755766 mph.
{earth,20}
5> Pid1 ! {eris,20}.
On eris, a fall of 20 meters yields a velocity of 12.65402255793022 mph.
{eris,20}
6> Pid1 ! {makemake,20}.
On makemake, a fall of 20 meters yields a velocity of 10.003883211552367 mph.
{makemake,20}
```

That's a lot more variety than its earth, moon, and mars predecessors!

Next Steps

While many applications just need a fast key/value store, ETS tables are far more flexible than the examples so far demonstrate. You can use Erlang's match specifications and ets:fun2ms to create more complex queries with ets:match and ets:select. You can delete rows (and tables) with ets:delete. The ets:first, ets:next, and ets:last functions let you traverse tables recursively.

Perhaps most important, you can also explore DETS, the disk-based term storage, which offers similar features but with tables stored on disk. It's slower, with a 2GB limit, but the data doesn't vanish when the controlling process stops.

You can dig deeper into ETS and DETS, but if your needs are more complex, and especially if you need to split data across multiple nodes, you should probably explore the Mnesia database.

ETS and DETS are discussed in Chapter 10 of *Erlang Programming*; Chapter 19 of *Programming Erlang*, 2nd Edition; Section 2.14 and Chapter 6 of *Erlang and OTP in Action*; and Chapter 25 of *Learn You Some Erlang For Great Good!*.

Storing Records in Mnesia

Mnesia is a database management system (DBMS) that comes with Erlang. It uses ETS and DETS underneath, but provides many more features than those components.

You should consider shifting from ETS (and DETS) tables to the Mnesia database if:

- You need to store and access data across a set of nodes, not just a single node.
- You don't want to have to think about whether you're going to store data in memory or on a disk (or both).
- You need to be able to roll back transactions if something goes wrong.
- You'd like a more approachable syntax for finding and joining data.
- Management prefers the sound of "database" to the sound of "tables."

You may even find yourself using ETS for some aspects of a project and Mnesia for others.

That isn't "amnesia," the forgetting, but "mnesia," the Greek word for memory.

Starting up Mnesia

If you want to store data on disk, you need to give Mnesia some information. Before you turn Mnesia on, you need to create a database, using the `mnesia:cre ate_schema/1` function. For now, because you'll be getting started using only the local node, that will look like the following:

```
1> mnesia:create_schema([node()]).
ok
```

By default, when you call `mnesia:create_schema/1`, Mnesia will store schema data in the directory you're in when you start it. If you look in the directory where you started Erlang, you'll see a new directory with a name like *Mnesia.nonode@nohost*. Initially, it holds a *LATEST.LOG* file and a *schema.DAT* file. The `node()` function just returns the identifier of the node you're on, which is fine when you're getting started.

(If you want to change where Mnesia stores data, you can start Erlang with some extra options: `erl -mnesia dir " path "`. The `path` will be the location where Mnesia keeps any disk-based storage.)

> If you start Mnesia without calling `mnesia:create_schema/1`, it will keep its schema in memory, and that schema will vanish if and when Mnesia stops.

Unlike ETS and DETS, which are always available, you need to turn Mnesia on:

```
2> mnesia:start().
ok
```

There's also an `mnesia:stop/0` function if you want to stop it.

> If you run Mnesia on a computer that goes to sleep, you may, when it wakes up, get odd messages like `Mnesia(nonode@nohost): ** WARNING ** Mnesia is overloaded: {dump_log, time_thres hold}`. Don't worry, it's a side effect of waking up, and your data should still be safe. You probably shouldn't run production systems on devices that go to sleep, of course.

Creating Tables

Like ETS, Mnesia's basic concept of a table is a collection of records. It also offers `set`, `ordered_set`, and `bag` options, just like those in ETS, but does not offer `duplicate_bag`.

Mnesia also wants to know more about your data than ETS. ETS pretty much takes data in tuples of any shape, counting only on there being a key it can use. The rest is up to you to interpret. Mnesia wants to know more about what you store, and takes a list of field names. The easy way to handle this is to define records and consistently use the field names from the records as Mnesia field names. There's even an easy way to pass the record names to Mnesia, using `record_info/2`.

The planemos table can work just as easily in Mnesia as in ETS, and some aspects of dealing with it will be easier. Example 10-8, which is in *ch10/ex7-mnesia*, shows how to set up the `planemo` table in Mnesia. The `setup/0` method creates a schema, then starts Mnesia, and then creates a table based on the `planemo` record type. Once the table is created, it writes the values from Table 10-1 to it.

Example 10-8. Setting up an Mnesia table of planemo properties

```erlang
-module(drop).
-export([setup/0]).
-include("records.hrl").

setup() ->
 mnesia:create_schema([node()]),
 mnesia:start(),
 mnesia:create_table(planemo, [{attributes, record_info(fields, planemo)}]),

 F = fun() ->
 mnesia:write(
  #planemo{ name=mercury, gravity=3.7, diameter=4878, distance_from_sun=57.9 }),
 mnesia:write(
  #planemo{ name=venus, gravity=8.9, diameter=12104, distance_from_sun=108.2 }),
 mnesia:write(
  #planemo{ name=earth, gravity=9.8, diameter=12756, distance_from_sun=149.6 }),
 mnesia:write(
  #planemo{ name=moon, gravity=1.6, diameter=3475, distance_from_sun=149.6 }),
 mnesia:write(
  #planemo{ name=mars, gravity=3.7, diameter=6787, distance_from_sun=227.9 }),
 mnesia:write(
  #planemo{ name=ceres, gravity=0.27, diameter=950, distance_from_sun=413.7 }),
 mnesia:write(
  #planemo{ name=jupiter, gravity=23.1, diameter=142796, distance_from_sun=778.3 }),
 mnesia:write(
  #planemo{ name=saturn, gravity=9.0, diameter=120660, distance_from_sun=1427.0 }),
 mnesia:write(
  #planemo{ name=uranus, gravity=8.7, diameter=51118, distance_from_sun=2871.0 }),
 mnesia:write(
  #planemo{ name=neptune, gravity=11.0, diameter=30200, distance_from_sun=4497.1 }),
 mnesia:write(
  #planemo{ name=pluto, gravity=0.6, diameter=2300, distance_from_sun=5913.0 }),
 mnesia:write(
  #planemo{ name=haumea, gravity=0.44, diameter=1150, distance_from_sun=6484.0 }),
 mnesia:write(
  #planemo{ name=makemake, gravity=0.5, diameter=1500, distance_from_sun=6850.0 }),
 mnesia:write(
  #planemo{ name=eris, gravity=0.8, diameter=2400, distance_from_sun=10210.0 })
 end,

 mnesia:transaction(F).
```

Apart from the setup, the key thing to note is that all of the writes are contained in a fun that is then passed to mnesia:transaction to be executed as a transaction. Mnesia will restart the transaction if there is other activity blocking it, so the code may get executed repeatedly before the transaction happens. Because of this, do not include any calls that create side effects to the function you'll be passing to mnesia:transaction, and don't try to catch exceptions on Mnesia functions within a transaction. If your function calls mnesia:abort/1 (probably because some condition for executing it wasn't met), the transaction will be rolled back, returning a tuple beginning with aborted instead of atomic.

 You may also want to explore the more flexible mnesia:activity/2 when you need to mix more kinds of tasks in a transaction.

Your interactions with Mnesia should be contained in transactions, especially when your database is shared across multiple nodes. The main mnesia:write, mne sia:read, and mnesia:delete methods work only within transactions, period. There are dirty_ methods, but every time you use them, especially to write data to the database, you're taking a risk.

 Just as in ETS, you can overwrite values by writing a new value with the same key as a previous entry.

If you want to check on how this function worked out, try the mnesia:table_info function, which can tell you more than you want to know. The following listing is abbreviated to focus on key results.

```
1> c(drop).
{ok,drop}
2> rr("records.hrl").
[planemo,tower]
3> drop:setup().
{atomic,ok}
4> mnesia:table_info(planemo,all).
[{access_mode,read_write},
 {active_replicas,[nonode@nohost]},
 {all_nodes,[nonode@nohost]},
 {arity,5},
 {attributes,[name,gravity,diameter,distance_from_sun]},
 ...
 {memory,541},
 {ram_copies,[nonode@nohost]},
 {record_name,planemo},
 {record_validation,{planemo,5,set}},
 {type,set},
 {size,14},
 ...]
```

You can see which nodes are involved in the table (nonode@nohost is the default for the current node). arity in this case is the count of fields in the record, and attributes tells you what their names are. `ram_copies` plus the name of the current node tells you that this table is stored in memory locally. It is, as in the ETS example, of type `set`, and there are 14 records.

 By default, Mnesia will store your table in RAM only (`ram_copies`) on the current node. This is speedy, but it means the data vanishes if the node crashes. If you specify `disc_copies` (note the spelling), Mnesia will keep a copy of the database on disk, but still use RAM for speed. You can also specify `disc_only_copies`, which will be slow. Unlike ETS, the table you create will still be around if the *process* that created it crashes, and will likely survive even a node crash so long as it wasn't only in RAM on a single node. By combining these options and (eventually) multiple nodes, you should be able to create fast and resilient systems.

The table is now set up, and you can start to use it. If you're running the Table Viewer, or start it with `observer:start()`, you can take a look at the contents of your Mnesia tables as well as your ETS tables. In the View menu, choose Mnesia Tables. The interface is similar to that for ETS tables.

Reading Data

Just like writes, you should wrap `mnesia:read` calls in a `fun`, which you then pass to `mnesia:transaction`. You can do that in the shell if you want to explore:

```
5> mnesia:transaction(fun() -> mnesia:read(planemo,neptune) end).
{atomic,[#planemo{name = neptune,gravity = 11.0,
                  diameter = 30300,distance_from_sun = 4497.1}]}
```

The result arrives as a tuple, which when successful contains `atomic` plus a list with the data from the table. The table data is packaged as a record, and you can get to its fields easily.

You can rewrite the `fall_velocity/2` function from Example 10-8 to use an Mnesia transaction instead of an ETS call. The ETS version looked like the following:

```
fall_velocity(Planemo, Distance) when Distance >= 0 ->
  P=hd(ets:lookup(planemos,Planemo)),
  math:sqrt(2 * P#planemo.gravity * Distance).
```

Line 2 of the Mnesia version is a bit different:

```
fall_velocity(Planemo, Distance) when Distance >= 0->
  {atomic, [P | _]}=mnesia:transaction(fun()->mnesia:read(planemo,Planemo) end),
  math:sqrt(2 * P#planemo.gravity * Distance).
```

Because Mnesia returns a tuple rather than a list, this code uses pattern matching to extract the first item in the list contained in the second item of the tuple (and throws away the tail of that list with _). This table is a set, so there will always be only one item there. Then the data, contained in P, can be used for the same calculation as before.

If you compile and run that code, you'll see a familiar result:

```
6> c(drop).
{ok,drop}
7> drop:fall_velocity(earth,20).
19.79898987322333
8> Pid1=spawn(mph_drop,mph_drop,[]).
<0.120.0>
9> Pid1 ! {earth,20}.
{earth,20}
On earth, a fall of 20 meters yields a velocity of 44.289078952755766 mph.
```

For these purposes, the simple mnesia:read is enough. You can tell Mnesia to build indexes for fields other than the key, and query those with mnesia:index_read.

If you want to delete records, you can run mnesia:delete/2, also inside of a transaction.

Query List Comprehensions

If Mnesia is really a database, it should be able to do more than key-value querying, right? It definitely can. You can use Erlang match specifications (as you can with ETS), but query list comprehensions (QLCs) are much more readable. They look like list comprehensions, which you saw in Chapter 7, but operate on Mnesia tables rather than lists.

Suppose you want to find all the planemos with gravity less than that of Earth. You could traverse the table with the mnesia:first and mnesia:next methods, but that seems like a lot of extra work. Instead, you can use the qlc:q function to hold a list comprehension and the qlc:e (or the equivalent but longer qlc:eval) function to process it. Then you run that inside of an mnesia:transaction call.

You can run query list comprehensions in the shell, but if you want to use them in modules you need to add -include_lib("stdlib/include/qlc.hrl"). to the declarations at the top of your module.

The simplest query list comprehension just returns all the values in the table. I've broken it out here on separate lines so that you can see how they interact:

```
mnesia:transaction(
  fun() ->
    qlc:e(
      qlc:q( [X || X <- mnesia:table(planemo)] )
    )
  end
)
```

As always, the mnesia:transaction function takes a fun as its argument. In this case, the fun contains a qlc:e function, which then contains a qlc:q function, where the real query is. It will build a list from the contents of the planemo table.

If you compact this a bit and run it in the shell, you'll see that the resulting list—wrapped in a transaction result tuple—contains the entire table.

```
10> mnesia:transaction( fun() -> qlc:e(qlc:q([X || X <- mnesia:table(planemo)]))
end).
{atomic,[#planemo{name = pluto,gravity = 0.6,
                  diameter = 2300,distance_from_sun = 5913.0},
        #planemo{name = saturn,gravity = 9.0,diameter = 120660,
                  distance_from_sun = 1427.0},
        #planemo{name = moon,gravity = 1.6,diameter = 3475,
                  distance_from_sun = 149.6},
        #planemo{name = mercury,gravity = 3.7,diameter = 4878,
                  distance_from_sun = 57.9},
        #planemo{name = earth,gravity = 9.8,diameter = 12756,
                  distance_from_sun = 149.6},
        #planemo{name = neptune,gravity = 11.0,diameter = 30200,
                  distance_from_sun = 4497.1},
        #planemo{name = makemake,gravity = 0.5,diameter = 1500,
                  distance_from_sun = 6850.0},
        #planemo{name = uranus,gravity = 8.7,diameter = 51118,
                  distance_from_sun = 2871.0},
        #planemo{name = ceres,gravity = 0.27,diameter = 950,
                  distance_from_sun = 413.7},
        #planemo{name = venus,gravity = 8.9,diameter = 12104,
                  distance_from_sun = 108.2},
        #planemo{name = mars,gravity = 3.7,diameter = 6787,
                  distance_from_sun = 227.9},
        #planemo{name = eris,gravity = 0.8,diameter = 2400,
                  distance_from_sun = 10210.0},
        #planemo{name = jupiter,gravity = 23.1,diameter = 142796,
                  distance_from_sun = 778.3},
        #planemo{name = haumea,gravity = 0.44,diameter = 1150,
                  distance_from_sun = 6484.0}]]}
```

You can add conditions to the query list comprehension. To find all of the planemos with gravity less than that of Earth's 9.8, you'd run:

```
mnesia:transaction(
  fun() ->
    qlc:e(
      qlc:q( [X || X <- mnesia:table(planemo),
```

```
            X#planemo.gravity < 9.8] )
      )
    end
  )
```

Compress and run that in the shell, and you'll get a shorter list of planemos where everything feels a little lighter.

```
11> mnesia:transaction( fun() -> qlc:e(qlc:q( [X || X <- mnesia:table(planemo),
  X#planemo.gravity < 9.8] )) end).
{atomic,[#planemo{name = pluto,gravity = 0.6,
                  diameter = 2300,distance_from_sun = 5913.0},
         #planemo{name = saturn,gravity = 9.0,diameter = 120660,
                  distance_from_sun = 1427.0},
         #planemo{name = moon,gravity = 1.6,diameter = 3475,
                  distance_from_sun = 149.6},
         #planemo{name = mercury,gravity = 3.7,diameter = 4878,
                  distance_from_sun = 57.9},
         #planemo{name = makemake,gravity = 0.5,diameter = 1500,
                  distance_from_sun = 6850.0},
         #planemo{name = uranus,gravity = 8.7,diameter = 51118,
                  distance_from_sun = 2871.0},
         #planemo{name = ceres,gravity = 0.27,diameter = 950,
                  distance_from_sun = 413.7},
         #planemo{name = venus,gravity = 8.9,diameter = 12104,
                  distance_from_sun = 108.2},
         #planemo{name = mars,gravity = 3.7,diameter = 6787,
                  distance_from_sun = 227.9},
         #planemo{name = eris,gravity = 0.8,diameter = 2400,
                  distance_from_sun = 10210.0},
         #planemo{name = haumea,gravity = 0.44,diameter = 1150,
                  distance_from_sun = 6484.0}]]}
```

That output still contains more information than might be necessary. You can modify the left side of the comprehension to cut things down, creating a tuple that is just the name and gravity of the planemo:

```
mnesia:transaction(
  fun() ->
    qlc:e(
      qlc:q( [{X#planemo.name, X#planemo.gravity} ||
              X <- mnesia:table(planemo),
              X#planemo.gravity < 9.8] )
    )
  end
)
```

The result is much trimmer:

```
12> mnesia:transaction( fun()->qlc:e(qlc:q( [ {X#planemo.name, X#planemo.gravity}
|| X<-mnesia:table(planemo), X#planemo.gravity < 9.8] )) end).
{atomic,[{pluto,0.6},
         {saturn,9.0},
```

```
{moon,1.6},
{mercury,3.7},
{makemake,0.5},
{uranus,8.7},
{ceres,0.27},
{venus,8.9},
{mars,3.7},
{eris,0.8},
{haumea,0.44}]]}
```

There are ways to reduce at least some of the syntax overhead here. It's not difficult, for example, to move the mnesia:transaction, fun definition, and qlc:e call to a function that takes the qlc:q function as its argument. In *Programming Erlang*, Joe Armstrong does just that to create a do function. You may want to break things up differently depending on your coding style and data structures.

You can use query list comprehensions on more than one table at a time, which is how you can create the equivalent of joins between tables, and it is also possible to use them on ETS tables.

This is just a brief introduction to Mnesia. It gets some coverage in all of the Erlang books, but eventually I hope it will get a book of its own, about as long as this one.

Mnesia is covered in Chapter 13 of *Erlang Programming* (O'Reilly); Chapter 20 of *Programming Erlang*, 2nd Edition (Pragmatic); Section 2.7 of *Erlang and OTP in Action* (Manning); and Chapter 29 of *Learn You Some Erlang For Great Good!* (No Starch Press).

CHAPTER 11

Getting Started with OTP

At this point, it might seem like you have all you need to create process-oriented projects with Erlang. You know how to create useful functions, can work with recursion, know the data structures Erlang offers, and probably most important, know how to create and manage processes. What more could you need?

Process-oriented programming is great, but the details matter. The basic Erlang tools are powerful, but can also lead you into frustrating mazes debugging race conditions that happen only once in a while. Mixing different programming styles can lead to incompatible expectations, and code that worked well in one environment may prove harder to integrate in another.

The Origins of OTP

Ericsson encountered these problems early, and created a library of code that eases them. OTP, originally the Open Telecom Platform, is useful for pretty much any large-scale project you want to do with Erlang, not just telecom work. It's included with Erlang, and though it isn't precisely part of the language, it is definitely part of the Erlang environment and helps to define Erlang programming culture. The boundaries of where Erlang ends and OTP begins aren't always clear, but the entry point is definitely behaviors. Your applications will combine processes built with behaviors and managed by supervisors in an OTP application.

So far, the lifecycle of the processes shown in the previous chapters has been pretty simple. If needed, they set up other resources or processes to get started. Once running, they listen for messages and process them, collapsing if they fail. Some of them might restart a failed process if needed.

OTP formalizes those activities, and a few more, into a set of behaviors (or behaviours—OTP was originally created with the British spelling). The most common behaviors are `gen_server` (generic server) and `supervisor`. `gen_statem` (state machine), `gen_fsm` (finite state machine), and `gen_event` are also available. The `application` behavior lets you package your OTP code into a single runnable (and updatable) system.

The behaviors predefine the mechanisms your code will use to create and interact with processes, and the compiler will warn you if you're missing some of them. Your code needs to handle the callbacks, specifying how to respond to particular kinds of events. OTP offers you some choices about how to structure your application as well.

 If you'd like a free one-hour video introduction to OTP, see Steve Vinoski's "Erlang's Open Telecom Platform (OTP) Framework" (*http://bitly.com/10Cif1r*). You probably already know the first half hour or so of it, but the review is excellent. In a very different style, if you'd like an explanation of why it's worth learning OTP and process-oriented development in general, Francesco Cesarini's slides (*http://bitly.com/10CiqKo*) work even without narration, especially the second half.

Creating Services with gen_server

Much of the work you think of as the core of a program—calculating results, storing information, and preparing replies—will fit neatly into the `gen_server` behavior. It provides a core set of methods that let you set up a process, respond to requests, end the process gracefully, and even pass state to a new process if this one needs to be upgraded in place.

Table 11-1 shows the methods you need to implement in a service that uses the `gen_server` behavior. For a simple service, the first two or three are the most important, and you may just use placeholder code for the rest.

Table 11-1. What calls and gets called in gen_server

Method	Triggered by	Does
init/1	gen_server:start_link	Sets up the process
handle_call/3	gen_server:call	Handles synchronous calls
handle_cast/2	gen_server:cast	Handles asynchronous calls
handle_info/2	random messages	Deals with non-OTP messages
terminate/2	failure or shutdown signal from supervisor	Cleans up the process
code_change/3	system libraries for code upgrades	Lets you switch out code without losing state

Appendix B shows a complete `gen_server` template from the Erlang emacs-mode, which is worth exploring in particular for the models it offers for the return value. (In

---

this context, a template is just a file full of code you can use as a base for creating your own code.) However, it's pretty big. Example 11-1, which you can find in *ch11/ex1-drop*, shows a less verbose example (based on the template) that you can use to get started. It mixes a simple calculation from way back in Example 2-1 with a counter like that in Example 8-4.

Example 11-1. A simple gen_server example based on the template from the Erlang mode for Emacs

```erlang
-module(drop).
-behaviour(gen_server).
-export([start_link/0]). % convenience call for startup
-export([init/1,
         handle_call/3,
         handle_cast/2,
         handle_info/2,
         terminate/2,
         code_change/3]). % gen_server callbacks
-define(SERVER, ?MODULE). % macro that just defines this module as server
-record(state, {count}). % simple counter state

%%% convenience method for startup
start_link() ->
        gen_server:start_link({local, ?SERVER}, ?MODULE, [], []).

%%% gen_server callbacks
init([]) ->
        {ok, #state{count=0}}.

handle_call(_Request, _From, State) ->
        Distance = _Request,
        Reply = {ok, fall_velocity(Distance)},
        NewState=#state{ count = State#state.count+1 },
        {reply, Reply, NewState}.

handle_cast(_Msg, State) ->
        io:format("So far, calculated ~w velocities.~n", [State#state.count]),
        {noreply, State}.

handle_info(_Info, State) ->
        {noreply, State}.

terminate(_Reason, _State) ->
        ok.

code_change(_OldVsn, State, _Extra) ->
        {ok, State}.

%%% Internal functions

fall_velocity(Distance) -> math:sqrt(2 * 9.8 * Distance).
```

The module name (drop) should be familiar from past examples. The second line is a -behaviour declaration specifying that this is going to be using the gen_server behavior. That declaration tells Erlang that it can expect this code to support the core callback functions of that behavior.

You can spell the -behaviour declaration -behavior if you prefer the American version. Erlang doesn't mind.

The -export declarations are pretty standard, though they break out the start_link/0 method into a separate declaration from the core gen_server methods. This isn't necessary, but it's a nice reminder that start_link isn't required for the gen_server behavior to work. (It *calls* gen_server code, but isn't a callback itself.)

The -define declaration is probably unfamiliar. Erlang lets you declare macros using -define. Macros are simple text replacements. This declaration tells the compiler that any time it encounters ?SERVER, it should replace it with ?MODULE. What is ?MODULE? That's a built-in macro that always refers to the name of the module it appears in. In this case, that means it will be processed into drop. (You may find cases where you want to register the server under a name other than the module name, but this is a workable default.)

The -record declaration should be familiar, though it contains only one field, to keep a count of the number of calls made. Many services will have more fields, including things like database connections, references to other processes, perhaps network information, and metadata specific to this particular service. It is also possible to have services with no state, which would be represented by an empty tuple here. As you'll see further down, every single gen_server function will reference the state.

The state record declaration is a good example of a record declaration you should make inside of a module and not declare through an included file. It is possible that you'll want to share state models across different gen_server processes, but it's easier to see what State should contain if the information is right there.

The first function in the sample, start_link/0, is *not* one of the required gen_server functions. Instead, it calls the gen_server's start_link function to start up the process. When you're just getting started, this is useful for testing. As you move toward production code, you may find it easier to leave these out and use other mechanisms.

The start_link/0 function uses the ?SERVER macro defined in the -define declaration as well as the built-in ?MODULE declaration.

```
%%% convenience method for startup
start_link() ->
        gen_server:start_link({local, ?SERVER}, ?MODULE, [], []).
```

The first argument, a tuple, opens with an atom that must be local or global, depending on whether you want the name of the process registered just with the local Erlang instance or with all associated nodes. The ?SERVER macro will be expanded to ?MODULE, which will itself be expanded to the name of the current module, and that will be used as the name for this process. The second argument is the name of the module, here identified with the ?MODULE macro, and then lists for arguments and options follow. In this case, they're both empty. Options can specify things like debugging, timeouts, and options for spawning the process.

 You may also see a form of gen_server:start_link with via as the atom in the first tuple. This lets you set up custom process registries, of which gproc is the best known. For more on that, see *https://github.com/uwiger/gproc*.

All of the remaining functions are part of the gen_server behavior. init/1 creates a new state record instance and sets its count field to zero—no velocities have yet been calculated. The two functions that do most of the work here are handle_call/3 and handle_cast/2. For this demonstration, handle_call/3 expects to receive a distance in meters and returns a velocity for a fall from that height on Earth, while handle_cast/2 is a trigger to report the number of velocities calculated.

handle_call/3 makes synchronous communications between Erlang processes simple.

```
handle_call(_Request, _From, State) ->
        Distance = _Request,
        Reply = {ok, fall_velocity(Distance)},
        NewState=#state{ count = State#state.count+1 },
        {reply, Reply, NewState}.
```

This extracts the Distance from the _Request, which isn't necessary except that I wanted to leave the variable names for the function the same as they were in the template. (handle_call(Distance, _From, State) would have been fine.) Your _Request is more likely to be a tuple or a list rather than a bare value, but this works for simple calls.

It then creates a reply based on sending that Distance to the simple fall_velocity/1 function at the end of the module. It then creates a NewState containing an incremented count. Then the atom reply, the Reply tuple containing the velocity, and the NewState containing the count get passed back.

Because the calculation is really simple, treating the drop as a simple synchronous call is perfectly acceptable. For more complex situations where you can't predict how long a response might take, you may want to consider responding with a `noreply` response and using the `_From` argument to send a response later. (There is also a `stop` response available that will trigger the `terminate/2` method and halt the process.)

 By default, OTP will time out any synchronous calls that take longer than 5 seconds to calculate. You can override this by making your call using `gen_server:call/3` to specify a timeout (in milliseconds) explicitly, or by using the atom `infinity`.

The `handle_cast/2` function supports asynchronous communications. It isn't supposed to return anything directly, though it does report `noreply` (or `stop`) and updated state. In the following example, it takes a very weak approach, but one that does well for a demonstration, calling `io:format/2` to report on the number of calls:

```
handle_cast(_Msg, State) ->
        io:format("So far, calculated ~w velocities.~n", [State#state.count]),
        {noreply, State}.
```

The state doesn't change, because asking for the number of times the process has calculated a fall velocity is not the same thing as actually calculating a fall velocity.

Until you have good reason to change them, you can leave `handle_info/2`, `terminate/2`, and `code_change/3` alone.

Making a `gen_server` process run and calling it looks a little different than starting the processes you saw in Chapter 8. Be very careful as you type this in: mistakes, as you'll see soon, can have unexpected effects:

```
1> c(drop).
{ok,drop}
2> drop:start_link().
{ok,<0.33.0>}
3> gen_server:call(drop, 20).
{ok,19.79898987322333}
4> gen_server:call(drop, 40).
{ok,28.0}
5> gen_server:call(drop, 60).
{ok,34.292856398964496}
6> gen_server:cast(drop, {}).
So far, calculated 3 velocities.
ok
```

The call to `drop:start_link()` sets up the process and makes it available. Then, you're free to use `gen_server:call` or `gen_server:cast` to send it messages and get responses.

While you can capture the pid, you don't have to keep it around to use the process. Because start_link returns a tuple, if you want to capture the pid you can do something like {ok, Pid} = drop:start_link().

Because of the way OTP calls gen_server functions, there's an additional bonus—or perhaps a hazard—in that you can update code on the fly. For example, I tweaked the fall_velocity/1 function to lighten Earth's gravity a little, using 9.1 as a constant instead of 9.8. Recompiling the code and asking for a velocity returns a different answer:

```
7> c(drop).
{ok,drop}
8> gen_server:call(drop, 60).
{ok,33.04542328371661}
```

This can be very convenient during the development phase, but be careful doing anything like this on a production machine. OTP has other mechanisms for updating code on the fly. There is also a built-in limitation to this approach: init gets called only when start_link sets up the service. It does not get called if you recompiled the code. If your new code requires any changes to the structure of its state, your code will break the next time it's called.

A Simple Supervisor

When you started the drop module from the shell, you effectively made the shell the supervisor for the module (though the shell doesn't really do any supervision). You can break the module easily:

```
9> gen_server:call(drop, -60).

=ERROR REPORT==== 2-Dec-2012::21:14:51 ===
** Generic server drop terminating
** Last message in was -60
** When Server state == {state,0}
** Reason for termination ==
** {badarith,[{math,sqrt,[-1176.0],[]},
             {drop,fall_velocity,1,[{file,"drop.erl"},{line,42}]},
             {drop,handle_call,3,[{file,"drop.erl"},{line,23}]},
             {gen_server,handle_msg,5,[{file,"gen_server.erl"},{line,588}]},
             {proc_lib,init_p_do_apply,3,
                        [{file,"proc_lib.erl"},{line,227}]}]}
** exception exit: badarith
     in function  math:sqrt/1
        called as math:sqrt(-1176.0)
     in call from drop:fall_velocity/1 (drop.erl, line 42)
     in call from drop:handle_call/3 (drop.erl, line 23)
     in call from gen_server:handle_msg/5 (gen_server.erl, line 588)
```

```
          in call from proc_lib:init_p_do_apply/3 (proc_lib.erl, line 227)
10> gen_server:call(drop, 60).
** exception exit: {noproc,{gen_server,call,[drop,60]}}
          in function  gen_server:call/2 (gen_server.erl, line 180)
```

The error message is nicely complete, even telling you the last message and the state, but when you go to call the service again on line 10, it isn't there. You can restart it with drop:start_link/0 again, but you're not always going to be watching your processes personally.

Instead, you want something that can watch over your processes and make sure they restart (or not) as appropriate. OTP formalizes the process management you saw in Example 8-10 with its supervisor behavior. Example B-2 in Appendix B shows a full template (again, from the Erlang mode for Emacs), but you can create a less verbose supervisor.

A basic supervisor needs to support only one callback function, init/1, and can also have a start_link function to fire it up. The return value of that init/1 function tells OTP which child processes your supervisor manages and how you want to handle their failures. A supervisor for the drop module might look like Example 11-2, which is in *ch11/ex2-drop-sup*.

Example 11-2. A simple supervisor

```
-module(drop_sup).
-behaviour(supervisor).
-export([start_link/0]). % convenience call for startup
-export([init/1]). % supervisor calls
-define(SERVER, ?MODULE).

%%% convenience method for startup
start_link() ->
        supervisor:start_link({local, ?SERVER}, ?MODULE, []).

%%% supervisor callback
init([]) ->
    SupFlags = #{strategy => one_for_one,
                 intensity => 1,
                 period => 5},

    Drop = #{id => 'drop',
             start => {'drop', start_link, []},
             restart => permanent,
             shutdown => 5000,
             type => worker,
             modules => ['drop']},

    {ok, {SupFlags, [Drop]}}.

%%% Internal functions (none here)
```

The init/1 function's job is to assemble a fairly complex data structure, held in two maps.

The first map defined in the template, SupFlags, defines how the supervisor should handle failure. The strategy of one_for_one tells OTP that it should create a new child process every time a process that is supposed to be permanent fails. You can also go with one_for_all, which terminates and restarts all of the processes the supervisor oversees when one fails, or rest_for_one, which restarts the process and any processes that began after the failed process started. There's also a simple_one_for_one optimized for the case where all child processes run identical code.

 When you're ready to take more direct control of how your processes respond to their environment, you might explore working with the dynamic functions supervisor:start/2, supervisor:terminate_child/2, supervisor:restart_child/2, and supervisor:delete_child/2, as well as the restart strategy simple_one_for_one.

The next two values define how often the worker processes can crash before terminating the supervisor itself. In this case, the default is one (intensity) restart every 5 (period) seconds. Customizing these values lets you handle a variety of conditions, but probably won't affect you much initially.

Those values, which here get combined into the map contained in SupFlags, apply to *all* of the workers managed by this supervisor. The next few lines define properties that apply to only one worker process, in this case the gen_server specified by Drop. It is designed to be a permanent service, so the supervisor should restart it when it fails. The supervisor can wait 2 seconds before shutting it off completely, and this worker is *only* a worker, not itself a supervisor. More complex OTP applications can contain trees of supervisors managing other supervisors, which themselves manage other supervisors or workers.

The Drop map might seem a bit repetitive, but it creates a complete set of information to get the Drop process started. First, it specifies an id, and then a tuple containing the name of the module containing the code, the function to use to start the process and a list of arguments. (Here there aren't any arguments.) Then the restart, shut down, and type are specified, and the final modules list identifies all the modules on which this process will depend. In this case, it all fits into a single module, so the list contains only the name of that module.

OTP wants to know the dependencies so that it can help you upgrade software in place. It's all part of the magic of keeping systems running without ever bringing them to a full stop.

Now that you have a supervisor process, you can set up the drop function by just calling the supervisor. However, running a supervisor from the shell using the start_link/0 function call creates its own set of problems; the shell is itself a supervisor, and will terminate processes that report errors. After a long error report, you'll find that both your worker and the supervisor have vanished.

In practice, this means that there are two ways to test supervised OTP processes (that aren't yet part of an application) directly from the shell. The first explicitly breaks the bond between the shell and the supervisor process by catching the pid of the supervisor (line 2) and then using the unlink/1 function to remove the link (line 3). Then you can call the process as usual with gen_server:call/2 and get answers. If you get an error (line 6), it'll be okay. The supervisor will restart the worker, and you can make new calls (line 7) successfully. The calls to whereis(drop) on lines 5 and 8 demonstrate that the supervisor has restarted drop with a new pid.

```
1> c(drop_sup).
{ok,drop_sup}
2>{ok, Pid} = drop_sup:start_link().
{ok,<0.80.0>}
3> unlink(Pid).
true
4> gen_server:call(drop, 60).
{ok,34.292856398964496}
5> whereis(drop).
<0.81.0>
6> gen_server:call(drop, -60).
** exception exit: {{badarith,
                      [{math,sqrt,[-1176.0],[]},
                       {drop,fall_velocity,1,[{file,"drop.erl"},{line,42}]},
                       {drop,handle_call,3,[{file,"drop.erl"},{line,23}]},
                       {gen_server,try_handle_call,4,
                           [{file,"gen_server.erl"},{line,615}]},
                       {gen_server,handle_msg,5,
                           [{file,"gen_server.erl"},{line,647}]},
                       {proc_lib,init_p_do_apply,3,
                           [{file,"proc_lib.erl"},{line,247}]}]},
                      {gen_server,call,[drop,-60]}}
     in function  gen_server:call/2 (gen_server.erl, line 204)
7>
=ERROR REPORT==== 16-Jan-2017::13:42:32 ===
** Generic server drop terminating
** Last message in was -60
** When Server state == {state,1}
```

```
** Reason for termination ==
** {badarith,[{math,sqrt,[-1176.0],[]},
              {drop,fall_velocity,1,[{file,"drop.erl"},{line,42}]},
              {drop,handle_call,3,[{file,"drop.erl"},{line,23}]},
              {gen_server,try_handle_call,4,
                          [{file,"gen_server.erl"},{line,615}]},
              {gen_server,handle_msg,5,[{file,"gen_server.erl"},{line,647}]},
              {proc_lib,init_p_do_apply,3,
                          [{file,"proc_lib.erl"},{line,247}]}]}

7> gen_server:call(drop, 60).
{ok,34.292856398964496}
8> whereis(drop).
<0.86.0>
```

The other approach leaves the link in place, but wraps the calls to gen_server/2 in a
catch statement. In this case, using catch just keeps the shell from ever receiving the
exception, so the supervisor remains untouched. You don't *have* to use catch to make
a call, as line 8 shows, but if the call fails, you'll have to restart the supervisor process
yourself. (Line 6 is also a bit split by the error message. Sometimes the timing will
make it look like the prompt disappeared. Don't worry, it hasn't.)

```
1> c(drop_sup).
{ok,drop_sup}
2> drop_sup:start_link().
{ok,<0.38.0>}
3> whereis(drop).
<0.39.0>
4> catch gen_server:call(drop, 60).
{ok,34.292856398964496}
5>
5> catch gen_server:call(drop, -60).
{'EXIT',{{badarith,[{math,sqrt,[-1176.0],[]},
                    {drop,fall_velocity,1,[{file,"drop.erl"},{line,42}]},
                    {drop,handle_call,3,[{file,"drop.erl"},{line,23}]},
                    {gen_server,handle_msg,5,
                                [{file,"gen_server.erl"},{line,588}]},
                    {proc_lib,init_p_do_apply,3,
                                [{file,"proc_lib.erl"},{line,227}]}]},
        {gen_server,call,[drop,-60]}}}
6>
=ERROR REPORT==== 2-Dec-2012::21:21:10 ===
** Generic server drop terminating
** Last message in was -60
** When Server state == {state,1}
** Reason for termination ==
** {badarith,[{math,sqrt,[-1176.0],[]},
              {drop,fall_velocity,1,[{file,"drop.erl"},{line,42}]},
              {drop,handle_call,3,[{file,"drop.erl"},{line,23}]},
              {gen_server,handle_msg,5,[{file,"gen_server.erl"},{line,588}]},
              {proc_lib,init_p_do_apply,3,
                          [{file,"proc_lib.erl"},{line,227}]}]}
```

```
catch gen_server:call(drop, 60).
{ok,34.292856398964496}
7> whereis(drop).
<0.43.0>
8> gen_server:call(drop, 60).
{ok,34.292856398964496}
```

 You can also tell the shell to stop worrying about such exceptions by issuing the shell command `catch_exception(true)`. However, that turns off the behavior for the entire shell, which may not be what you want. (It will return `false`, the previous setting for that property. Don't worry, it did set it to `true`.)

You can also open Process Manager or Observer and whack away at worker processes through the Kill option on the Trace menu and watch them reappear.

This works, but is only the tiniest taste of what supervisors can do. They can create child processes dynamically, and manage their lifecycles in greater detail. Experimenting with supervisors is the best way to learn about them.

Packaging an Application

OTP also lets you package sets of components into an application. While stopping and starting OTP workers and supervisors may be easier than dealing with processes directly, OTP's facilities for describing applications will lead you down a path to much easier starting, updating, administering, and (if you must) stopping your projects.

Erlang applications include two extra components beyond the workers, supervisors, and related files they need. The application resource file, also known as an app file, provides a lot of metadata about your application. You'll also need a module with the behavior `application` to define starting and stopping.

 If you're on a Mac, the file extension for the *.app* file will disappear and the operating system will think it's some kind of broken Mac application. Don't worry. It'll still work in Erlang, though the Mac won't know what to do if you double-click on it.

The app file is a large tuple but is easier to read than the one returned by a supervisor's `init/1` functions. Example 11-3, in *ch11/ex3-drop-app*, shows a minimal app file, placed in an *ebin* subdirectory, that sets up this simple drop application.

Example 11-3. drop.app, an application resource file, or app file, for the drop program

```
{application, drop,
[{description, "Dropping objects from towers"},
{vsn, "0.0.1"},
{modules, [drop, drop_sup,drop_app]},
{registered,[drop, drop_sup]},
{applications, [kernel,stdlib]},
{mod, {drop_app,[]} }]}.
```

The first line identifies this as an application named `drop`, and then a list of arguments provides more information:

- The `description` is a (sometimes) human-friendly description of what's here. `vsn` is a version number, which in this case is tiny.

- `modules` lists the modules that make up the application, in this case `drop`, `drop_sup`, and `drop_app`.

- `registered` lists modules that are publicly visible, again `drop` and `drop_sup`.

- `applications` lists the required applications on which this application depends, and the `kernel` and `stdlib` seem to be the minimal standard set.

- `mod` has a tuple that points to the module with the `application` behavior. It can take a list of arguments that will go to the `start/2` function of the module, though there aren't any here.

That module is trivial even compared to the other OTP code you've seen, as shown in Example 11-4, which is also in *ch11/ex3-drop-app*. (Example B-3 shows a fuller template.)

Example 11-4. The application module for the drop program

```
-module(drop_app).
-behaviour(application).
-export([start/2, stop/1]).

start(_Type, _StartArgs) ->
  drop_sup:start_link().

stop(_State) ->
  ok.
```

The only thing you really have to do is start up the supervisors for your application in the `start/2` function. In this case there's only one, and the `_Type` and `_StartArgs` don't matter.

Running this application from the shell will require one bit of extra effort on your part. You'll need to compile drop_app, of course, but you'll also need to tell Erlang about the *ebin* directory containing the *drop.app* file, as shown on line 2. (OTP expects it to be there, but will give you "no such file or directory" errors if you don't tell Erlang about the directory.)

```
1> c(drop_app).
{ok,drop_app}
2> code:add_path("ebin/").
true
3> application:load(drop).
ok
4> application:loaded_applications().
[{kernel,"ERTS  CXC 138 10","2.15.2"},
 {drop,"Dropping objects from towers","0.0.1"},
 {stdlib,"ERTS  CXC 138 10","1.18.2"}]
5> application:start(drop).
ok
6> gen_server:call(drop, 60).
{ok,34.292856398964496}
```

Once Erlang knows where to look, you can use the application module's functions to load the application and check that Erlang found it. Once you start the application, you can go ahead and make calls to it with gen_server:call. Because the supervisor is bound to an application, you don't need to worry about the shell shutting you down. You can go ahead and break the drop calculation process with a negative value, and the supervisor will just fire it back up.

```
7> whereis(drop).
<0.45.0>
8> gen_server:call(drop, -60).

=ERROR REPORT==== 2-Dec-2012::21:25:38 ===
** Generic server drop terminating
** Last message in was -60
** When Server state == {state,1}
** Reason for termination ==
** {badarith,[{math,sqrt,[-1176.0],[]},
             {drop,fall_velocity,1,[{file,"drop.erl"},{line,42}]},
             {drop,handle_call,3,[{file,"drop.erl"},{line,23}]},
             {gen_server,handle_msg,5,[{file,"gen_server.erl"},{line,588}]},
             {proc_lib,init_p_do_apply,3,
                       [{file,"proc_lib.erl"},{line,227}]}]}
** exception exit: {{badarith,
                    [{math,sqrt,[-1176.0],[]},
                     {drop,fall_velocity,1,
                         [{file,"drop.erl"},{line,42}]},
                     {drop,handle_call,3,
                         [{file,"drop.erl"},{line,23}]},
                     {gen_server,handle_msg,5,
                         [{file,"gen_server.erl"},{line,588}]},
```

```
              {proc_lib,init_p_do_apply,3,
                    [{file,"proc_lib.erl"},{line,227}]}]},
              {gen_server,call,[drop,-60]}}
     in function  gen_server:call/2 (gen_server.erl, line 180)
9> gen_server:call(drop, 60).
{ok,34.292856398964496}
10> whereis(drop).
<0.49.0>
```

There is much, much more to learn. OTP deserves a book or several all on its own. Hopefully this chapter provides you with enough information to try some things out and understand those books. However, the gap between what this chapter can reasonably present and what you need to know to write solid OTP-based programs is... vast.

 You can learn more about working with OTP basics in Chapters 11 and 12 of *Erlang Programming* (O'Reilly); Chapters 22 and 23 of *Programming Erlang*, 2nd Edition (Pragmatic); Chapter 4 of *Erlang and OTP in Action* (Manning); and Chapters 14 through 20 of *Learn You Some Erlang For Great Good!* (No Starch Press). You can move much deeper into OTP with *Designing for Scalability with Erlang/OTP* (O'Reilly).

CHAPTER 12

Next Steps Through Erlang

Hopefully you now feel comfortable writing basic Erlang programs, and understand roughly how modules and processes build into programs. You should be ready to experiment with writing Erlang code, but more importantly, you should be ready to explore other resources for mastering Erlang and its many powerful libraries. There's a lot to explore!

Moving Beyond the Erlang Shell

The Erlang shell is a great place to test code and to poke and prod Erlang code. You'll likely spend a lot more time in the shell if you keep using Erlang, but the way you use it may change.

You can compile and run Erlang code outside of the shell, which makes it much easier to integrate Erlang work with tools you typically use to manage code and related resources. Erlang's `make` module is a common place to start, letting you create *Emakefile* files that provide instruction to the `erl -make` command. The `escript` command, described at *http://erlang.org/doc/man/escript.html*, will let you run Erlang from the command line in a variety of different environments.

If you want to automate your Erlang builds further, you may want to explore rebar3 (*https://www.rebar3.org/*). You can mix rebar3 with other tools to apply the strengths of each.

If you want to use Erlang from an IDE, you may want to explore *http://erlide.org/*, a set of tools for working with Erlang in Eclipse. Emacs users will want to explore the Erlang mode.

Distributed Computing

Almost everything you've learned in this book points toward a computing model that makes it easy to distribute programs across a network of Erlang nodes. Setting up a set of nodes isn't that difficult. It may even be too easy (in some ways) to let security-obsessed administrators sleep easily. *Designing for Scalability with Erlang/OTP* (O'Reilly) explores this in greater depth.

Before you set up large sets of nodes, you'll want to know much more about how Erlang schedules code to run, how messages get passed among nodes, and how to administer Erlang nodes remotely. All of that info is out there, providing the foundation on which tools like OTP and Mnesia can build.

Processing Binary Data

Erlang includes a binary data type, binary operators, and a variety of libraries for processing binary data. If you need to build network protocols that handle bits on the wire, or ASN.1 data, for example, Erlang offers powerful tools for getting information into and out of binary form. If you see numbers or strings enclosed in << and >>, you've encountered Erlang's tools for handling binary data. They allow you to specify, pattern match, and process binary data structures.

Input and Output

Chapters 4 and 5 introduced you to the `io:format` functions in the context of presenting information in the shell. The `io` module offers much more, however, for reading and writing data, and the `file`, `filename`, `filelib`, and `io_lib` modules give you the tools you need to get into and out of files. If networking is more your style, you'll want to explore the `gen_tcp`, `gen_udp`, and `inet` modules.

Testing, Analyzing, and Refactoring

Functional programming approaches should, once you get used to them, make it easier to create clean code. However, it is always possible to tie yourself in knots, especially as you move toward solving more complex problems than the ones presented in this book.

Unit testing is one approach to making sure that your code keeps working as you move forward. Focused on small components of your programs that should be able to reliably return a set of correct outputs from a given set of inputs, unit testing can both help to tell you when you've made your code work and warn you when it breaks. Erlang includes the EUnit framework for unit testing and the Common Test framework for system testing.

Erlang also includes Dialyzer, the discrepancy analyzer for Erlang, which can help you catch basic errors of sending wrongly typed data, code that never gets called, and similar issues that compilers for statically typed languages are usually good at catching. Erlang also includes profilers and coverage tools; you should explore the `eprof`, `fprof`, and `cover` modules, and the `cprof` tool.

If you're excited about refactoring code—once you have more of it—you may want to explore Wrangler (*https://github.com/RefactoringTools/wrangler*). It allows you to explore your code and automate a wide variety of common program modifications.

Networking and the Web

Erlang is a natural match for a world of web programming in which the number of users is constantly increasing, data needs to move smoothly among nodes, and customers are starting to expect critical web applications to work as reliably as the telephone system. Most web applications are large pipelines of data, well-suited for Erlang's strengths.

Several Erlang frameworks let you build web applications. Cowboy (*https://github.com/ninenines/cowboy*), Yaws (*http://yaws.hyber.org/*), and Mochiweb (*https://github.com/mochi/mochiweb*) are web servers written in Erlang. They offer environments that should be fairly familiar to anyone building web applications. Yaws lets you mix Erlang code with HTML (and other) templates, making it fairly easy to get a website or application together on an Erlang foundation. For a more comprehensive framework that can run with any of these, take a look at Nitrogen (*http://nitrogenproject.com/*).

If you have fallen for the siren song of REST-based service development, you may also want to explore Webmachine (*https://github.com/basho/webmachine/*), a toolkit for HTTP processing that brings you very close to the core of the web's foundation protocol. Even if you don't end up using it, exploring its flow diagram (*https://github.com/basho/webmachine/wiki/Diagram*) will teach you a lot about what's involved in processing a web request.

Data Storage

You already have ETS, DETS, and Mnesia. What else might you need?

Many people are using Erlang without knowing they are using it, as they interact with the popular NoSQL databases CouchDB (*http://couchdb.apache.org/*) and Riak (*http://basho.com/products/#riak*). Their Erlang underpinnings make them easy to distribute and manage, and they've both reached large and growing audiences. For a great brief intro to them (and five other database options), you should explore *Seven Databases in Seven Weeks* (Pragmatic Programmers). It won't teach you much about using them with Erlang, but it will give you a solid foundation that will help you explore their Erlang interfaces once their broad approaches make sense to you.

Many other databases have Erlang interfaces, and there is support for the classic ODBC connections.

Extending Erlang

If you need to wring out every drop of performance on a complex task, or want to avoid rewriting a library written in a language other than Erlang, you'll want to explore Erlang's tools for connecting with other programming languages. *Erlang Programming* (O'Reilly) explores Java, C, and Ruby connections, but also notes approaches you can use to connect with .NET languages, Python, Perl, PHP, Haskell, Scheme, and Emacs Lisp. You'll also want to examine native implemented functions (NIFs) and drivers.

Languages Built on Erlang

Erlang may put the fun in functional programming, but its structures may feel brittle if you're used to the flexibility that many other languages provide. Elixir (*http://elixir-lang.org/*) combines the Erlang runtime system with a very different (Rubyish) syntax more focused on polymorphism, metaprogramming, and associative data structures. If you prefer Lisp approaches to functional programming, you might want to explore Lisp Flavored Erlang (*http://lfe.io/*).

Erlang's runtime model and tools are powerful and unique, and there may be other great ideas coming that will let you apply them to work that might not seem on the surface to be written in Erlang.

Community

As you learn more about Erlang, you'll find a community happy to help you at every level. The erlang-questions mailing list welcomes beginners. During the writing of this book, I found its archives incredibly valuable. You can find subscription and archive information at *http://erlang.org/mailman/listinfo/erlang-questions*, and you will probably run into its archives regularly if you do searches on Erlang topics. If you prefer live chat to email, there is also an #erlang IRC channel on freenode (*http://freenode.net*) and an Erlang slack (*https://erlanger.slack.com*).

If you prefer "real" live chat to the internet, Erlang has a thriving conference circuit. For completely Erlang-focused venues, check out Erlang Factory (*http://www.erlangfactory.com/*), which produces a number of shows around the world, including the Erlang User Conference. The Association for Computing Machinery (ACM)'s Special

Interest Group on Programming Languages (SIGPLAN) also holds an Erlang workshop (*http://www.erlang.org/workshop/*).

There are also a lot of more informal "Erlounges" in a wide variety of locations, and many larger conferences, like the Open Source Convention (OSCON), include Erlang sessions and tutorials.

If you want to explore Erlang code, there's lots of it on GitHub; you can look around at the most active projects by visiting *https://github.com/languages/Erlang*.

Sharing the Gospel of Erlang

It may seem easy to argue for Erlang. The broad shift from single computers to networked and distributed systems of multiprocessor-based computing gives the Erlang environment a tremendous advantage over practically every other environment out there. More and more of the computing world is starting to face exactly the challenges that Erlang was built to address. Veterans of those challenges may find themselves breathing a sigh of relief when they discover Erlang. They can stop pondering toolsets that tried too hard to carry single-system approaches into a multisystem world.

At the same time, though, I'd encourage you to consider a bit of wisdom from Joe Armstrong (*http://erlang.org/pipermail/erlang-questions/2012-October/069626.html*): "New technologies have their best chance a) immediately after a disaster or b) at the start of a new project."

While it is possible you're reading this because a project you're working on has had a disaster (or you suspect it will have one soon), it's easiest to apply Erlang to new projects, preferably projects where the inevitable beginner's mistakes won't create new disasters.

Find projects that look like fun to you, and that you can share within your organization or with the world. There's no better way to show off the power of a programming language and environment than to build great things with it!

An Erlang Parts Catalog

Like every language, Erlang has drawers full of parts that are fun to peruse. These are a very few of the more common ones. For much much more, see *http://bitly.com/10CiiKR.*

Shell Commands

You can use most Erlang functions from the shell, but these are ones that are exclusive to the shell.

Table A-1. Erlang shell commands

Command	Action
q()	Quits the shell *and* the Erlang runtime
c(file)	Compiles the specified Erlang file
b()	Displays all variable bindings
f()	Clears all variable bindings
f(X)	Clears specified variable binding
h()	Prints the history list of commands
e(N)	Repeats the command on line N
v(N)	The return value of line N
catch_exception(boolean)	Sets how strict the shell will be in passing errors
rd(Name,Definition)	Defines a record type Name with contents specified by Definition
rr(File)	Defines record types based on the contents of File
rf()	Clears all record definitions. Can also clear specific definitions
rl()	Lists all current record definitions
pwd()	Gets the present working directory

Command	Action
ls()	Lists files at the current location
cd(Directory)	Changes to the specified Directory

Reserved Words

There are a few Erlang terms you can't use outside of their intended context.

The Erlang compiler will wonder what you're trying to do if you use certain keywords as atoms or function names. It will try to treat your atoms as if they were code, and you can get very strange errors. After all, you should be able to have something called band, right? Unfortunately, no. band is one of the reserved words.

Table A-2. Reserved words, which require careful use

after	and	andalso	band	begin	bnot	bor	bsl	bsr	bxor
case	catch	cond	div	end	fun	if	let	not	of
or	orelse	query	receive	rem	try	when	xor		

For function names, the answer is simple: use something else. If you want to use these as atoms, however, you can. You just need to enclose the offending reserved word in single quotes: 'receive', for example.

While they aren't reserved words, there are also a few atoms commonly used in return values. It's probably best to use them only in circumstances where they're normally expected.

Table A-3. Commonly used return value atoms

Atom	Means
ok	Normal exit to a method. (Does *not* mean that whatever you asked for succeeded.)
error	Something went wrong. Typically accompanied by a larger explanation.
undefined	A value hasn't been assigned yet. Common in record instances.
reply	A reply is included with some kind of return value.
noreply	No return value is included. A response of some sort may come, however, from other communication.
stop	Used in OTP to signal that a server should stop, and triggers the terminate function.
ignore	Returned by OTP supervisor process that can't start a child.

Operators

Table A-4. Logical (Boolean) operators

Operator	Description
and	logical and
or	logical or
xor	logical xor
not	unary logical not

The not operator is processed first.

andalso and orelse are also boolean operators for logical and and logical or, but they are short-circuit operators. If they don't need to process all the possibilities in their arguments, they stop at the first one that gives them a definite answer.

Table A-5. Term comparison operators

Operator	Description
==	equal to
/=	not equal to
=<	less than or equal to
<	less than
>=	greater than or equal to
>	greater than
=:=	exactly equal to
=/=	exactly not equal to

You can compare elements of different types in Erlang. The relationship of types from "least" to "greatest" is:

number < atom < reference < fun < port < pid < tuple < list < bit string

Within number, you can compare integers and floats except with the more specific =:= and =/= operators, both of which will return false when you compare numbers of different types.

You can also compare tuples even when they contain different numbers of values. Erlang will go through the tuples from left to right and evaluate on the first value that returns a clear answer.

Table A-6. Arithmetic operators

Operator	Description
+	unary + (positive)
-	unary - (negative)
+	addition
-	subtraction
*	multiplication
/	floating point division
div	integer division
rem	integer remainder of X/Y

Table A-7. Binary operators

Operator	Description
bnot	unary bitwise not
band	bitwise and
bor	bitwise or
bxor	arithmetic bitwise xor
bsl	arithmetic bitshift left
bsr	bitshift right

Table A-8. Operator precedence, from highest to lowest

Operator	Associativity
:	
#	
Unary + - bnot not	
/ * div rem band and	Left associative
+ - bor bxor bsl bsr or xor	Left associative
++ --	Right associative +
== /= =< < >= > =:= =/=+	
andalso	
orelse	
= !	Right associative
catch	

The highest priority operator in an expression is evaluated first. Erlang evaluates operators with the same priority by following associative paths. (Left associative operators go left to right, right associative operators go right to left.)

Guard Components

Erlang allows only a limited subset of functions and other features in guard expressions, going well beyond a "no side effects" rule to keep a simple subset of possibilities. The list of allowed components includes the following:

- `true`
- Other constants (regarded as `false`)
- Term comparisons (Table A-5)
- Arithmetic expressions (Tables A-6 and A-7)
- Boolean expressions and short-circuit expressions (`andalso` and `orelse`)
- The following functions: `abs/1`, `bit_size/1`, `byte_size/1`, `element/2`, `float/1`, `hd/1`, `is_atom/1`, `is_binary/1`, `is_bitstring/1`, `is_boolean/1`, `is_float/1`, `is_function/1`, `is_function/2`, `is_integer/1`, `is_list/1`, `is_map/1`, `is_num ber/1`, `is_pid/1`, `is_port/1`, `is_record/2`, `is_record/3`, `is_reference/1`, `is_tuple/1`, `length/1`, `map_size/1`, `node/0`, `round/1`, `self/0`, `size/1`, `tl/1`, `trunc/1`, `tuple_size/1`

Common Functions

Table A-9. Mathematical functions

Function	Use
`math:pi/0`	The constant pi
`math:sin/1`	Sine
`math:cos/1`	Cosine
`math:tan/1`	Tangent
`math:asin/1`	Inverse sine (arcsine)
`math:acos/1`	Inverse cosine (arcosine)
`math:atan/1`	Inverse tangent (arctangent)
`math:atan2/2`	Arctangent that understands quadrants
`math:sinh/1`	Hyperbolic sine
`math:cosh/1`	Hyperbolic cosine
`math:tanh/1`	Hyperbolic tangent
`math:asinh/1`	Hyperbolic arcsine
`math:acosh/1`	Hyperbolic arccosine
`math:atanh/1`	Hyperbolic arctangent
`math:exp/1`	Exponential function

Function	Use
math:log/1	Natural logarithm (base e)
math:log10/1	Logarithm (base 10)
math:pow/2	First argument to the second argument power
math:sqrt/1	Square root
math:erf/1	Error function
math:erfc/1	Complementary error function

Arguments for all trigonometric functions are expressed in radians. To convert degrees to radians, divide by 180 and multiply by pi.

 The erf/1 and erfc/1 functions may not be implemented in Windows. The Erlang documentation also warns more broadly that "Not all functions are implemented on all platforms," but these come directly from the C language libraries.

Table A-10. Approachable higher-order functions for processing lists

function	Returns	Use
lists:foreach/2	ok	Side effects specified in function
lists:map/2	new list	Apply function to list values
lists:filter/2	subset	Creating list where function returns true
lists:all/2	boolean	Returns true if function true for all values, otherwise false
lists:any/2	boolean	Returns true if function true for any values, otherwise false
lists:takewhile/2	subset	Collects the head of the list until the function is true
lists:dropwhile/2	subset	Deletes the head of the list until the function is true
lists:foldl/3	accumulator	Passes function list value and accumulator, forward-through list
lists:foldr/3	accumulator	Passes function list value and accumulator, backward-through list
lists:partition/3	tuple of two lists	Split list based on function

Chapter 7 describes these in greater detail.

Strings and Formatting

Table A-11. Simple control sequences for io:format and error_logger functions

Sequence	Produces
~p	Value, pretty-printed
~w	Value, no indentation
~s	Contents of a string

Sequence	Produces
~c	ASCII character corresponding to a number
~tc	Unicode character corresponding to a number
~i	Ignores that item
~n	Newline (doesn't reference argument list)

Table A-12. Escape sequences for strings

Sequence	Produces
\"	double quote
\'	single quote
\\	backslash
\b	backspace
\d	delete
\e	escape
\f	form feed
\n	newline
\r	carriage return
\s	space
\t	tab
\v	vertical tab
\XYZ, \YZ, \Z	character with octal representation XYZ, YZ or Z
\xXY	character in hex
\x{X...}	characters in hex, where X... is one or more hexadecimal characters
^a...\^z or ^A...\^Z	control-A to control-Z

Table A-13. Common string-processing functions

Function	Returns
string:len/1	Length of the string (traverses string, so slows with big ones)
length/1	Length of the string (traverses string, so slows with big ones)
string:concat/2	A single string containing the two parts from the arguments
lists:concat/1	A single string containing all the parts from the arguments
lists:append/1-2	A single string containing all the parts from the arguments
lists:nth/2	The character at the specified position
hd/1	First character of the string
string:chr/2	The position where the specified character first appears
string:str/2	The position of a substring in a string
string:substr/2-3	A segment from a string at a given position of a given length

Function	Returns
string:sub_string/2-3	A segment from a string between two positions
string:tokens/2	A list of pieces from a string broken at the specified separators
string:join/2	A string made from the list of pieces with specified separators added
string:words/1-2	The number of words in the string
string:chars/2-3	A string that repeats a given character a given number of times
string:copies/2	A string that repeats a given string a given number of times
string:strip/1-3	A string with leading and/or trailing whitespace (or specified characters) removed
string:left/2-3	A string of a specified length, padded with spaces on the right if needed
string:right/2-3	A string of a specified length, padded with spaces on the left if needed
string:centre/2-3	A string of a specified length, padded with spaces on the left *and* right if needed
lists:reverse/1-2	A string in backwards order
string:to_float/1	The float contents of the string, plus leftovers, or an error tuple
string:to_integer/1	The integer contents of the string, plus leftovers, or an error tuple
string:to_lower/1	A version of the string with all uppercase (Latin-1) characters converted to lowercase
string:to_upper/1	A version of the string with all lowercase (Latin-1) characters converted to uppercase
integer_to_list/1-2	A string version of an integer, optionally in a specified base
float_to_list/1	A string version of a float
erlang:fun_to_list/1	A string version of a fun
list_to_atom/1	An atom version of a string

Note: I wrote a single wrapper module that assembles Erlang's tools for working with strings into one place. For more, visit *https://github.com/simonstl/erlang-simple-string*.

Data Types for Documentation and Analysis

Table A-14. Basic Data Types for -spec and EDoc

atom()	binary()	float()	fun()	integer()	list()	tuple()
union()	node()	number()	string()	char()	byte()	[] (nil)
any()	none()	pid()	port()	reference()		

For more, see *http://www.erlang.org/doc/reference_manual/typespec.html*.

OTP Templates

These are the full templates for gen_server, supervisor, and application from the Emacs mode for Erlang. Some pieces are more useful than others, but seeing the full set of expected responses can be useful. (In this context, a template is just a file full of code you can use as a base for creating your own code.)

 Remember, the noreply atom doesn't mean "there will never be a reply" but rather that "this response isn't a reply."

Example B-1. A gen_server template from the Erlang mode for Emacs

```
%%% @author $author
%%% @copyright (C) $year, $company
%%% @doc
%%%
%%% @end
%%% Created : $fulldate
%%%-------------------------------------------------------------------
-module($basename).

-behaviour(gen_server).

%% API
-export([start_link/0]).

%% gen_server callbacks
-export([init/1, handle_call/3, handle_cast/2, handle_info/2,
         terminate/2, code_change/3]).

-define(SERVER, ?MODULE).
```

```erlang
-record(state, {}).

%%%===================================================================
%%% API
%%%===================================================================

%%--------------------------------------------------------------------
%% @doc
%% Starts the server
%%
%% @spec start_link() -> {ok, Pid} | ignore | {error, Error}
%% @end
%%--------------------------------------------------------------------
start_link() ->
    gen_server:start_link({local, ?SERVER}, ?MODULE, [], []).

%%%===================================================================
%%% gen_server callbacks
%%%===================================================================

%%--------------------------------------------------------------------
%% @private
%% @doc
%% Initializes the server
%%
%% @spec init(Args) -> {ok, State} |
%%                     {ok, State, Timeout} |
%%                     ignore |
%%                     {stop, Reason}
%% @end
%%--------------------------------------------------------------------
init([]) ->
    {ok, #state{}}.

%%--------------------------------------------------------------------
%% @private
%% @doc
%% Handling call messages
%%
%% @spec handle_call(Request, From, State) ->
%%                                   {reply, Reply, State} |
%%                                   {reply, Reply, State, Timeout} |
%%                                   {noreply, State} |
%%                                   {noreply, State, Timeout} |
%%                                   {stop, Reason, Reply, State} |
%%                                   {stop, Reason, State}
%% @end
%%--------------------------------------------------------------------
handle_call(_Request, _From, State) ->
    Reply = ok,
    {reply, Reply, State}.
```

```
%%--------------------------------------------------------------------
%% @private
%% @doc
%% Handling cast messages
%%
%% @spec handle_cast(Msg, State) -> {noreply, State} |
%%                                  {noreply, State, Timeout} |
%%                                  {stop, Reason, State}
%% @end
%%--------------------------------------------------------------------
handle_cast(_Msg, State) ->
    {noreply, State}.


%%--------------------------------------------------------------------
%% @private
%% @doc
%% Handling all non call/cast messages
%%
%% @spec handle_info(Info, State) -> {noreply, State} |
%%                                   {noreply, State, Timeout} |
%%                                   {stop, Reason, State}
%% @end
%%--------------------------------------------------------------------
handle_info(_Info, State) ->
    {noreply, State}.


%%--------------------------------------------------------------------
%% @private
%% @doc
%% This function is called by a gen_server when it is about to
%% terminate. It should be the opposite of Module:init/1 and do any
%% necessary cleaning up. When it returns, the gen_server terminates
%% with Reason. The return value is ignored.
%%
%% @spec terminate(Reason, State) -> void()
%% @end
%%--------------------------------------------------------------------
terminate(_Reason, _State) ->
    ok.


%%--------------------------------------------------------------------
%% @private
%% @doc
%% Convert process state when code is changed
%%
%% @spec code_change(OldVsn, State, Extra) -> {ok, NewState}
%% @end
%%--------------------------------------------------------------------
code_change(_OldVsn, State, _Extra) ->
    {ok, State}.
```

```
%%%=====================================================================
%%% Internal functions
%%%=====================================================================
```

Example B-2. A supervisor template from the Erlang mode for Emacs

```
%%%-------------------------------------------------------------------
%%% @author $author
%%% @copyright (C) $year, $company
%%% @doc
%%%
%%% @end
%%% Created : $fulldate
%%%-------------------------------------------------------------------
-module($basename).

-behaviour(supervisor).

%% API
-export([start_link/0]).

%% Supervisor callbacks
-export([init/1]).

-define(SERVER, ?MODULE).

%%%=====================================================================
%%% API functions
%%%=====================================================================

%%-------------------------------------------------------------------
%% @doc
%% Starts the supervisor
%%
%% @spec start_link() -> {ok, Pid} | ignore | {error, Error}
%% @end
%%-------------------------------------------------------------------
start_link() ->
    supervisor:start_link({local, ?SERVER}, ?MODULE, []).

%%%=====================================================================
%%% Supervisor callbacks
%%%=====================================================================

%%-------------------------------------------------------------------
%% @private
%% @doc
%% Whenever a supervisor is started using supervisor:start_link/[2,3],
%% this function is called by the new process to find out about
%% restart strategy, maximum restart frequency and child
%% specifications.
%%
```

```
%% @spec init(Args) -> {ok, {SupFlags, [ChildSpec]}} |
%%                      ignore |
%%                      {error, Reason}
%% @end
%%--------------------------------------------------------------------
init([]) ->
    SupFlags = #{strategy => one_for_one,
                 intensity => 1,
                 period => 5},

    AChild = #{id => 'AName',
               start => {'AModule', start_link, []},
               restart => permanent,
               shutdown => 5000,
               type => worker,
               modules => ['AModule']},

    {ok, {SupFlags, [AChild]}}.


%%%===================================================================
%%% Internal functions
%%%===================================================================
```

Example B-3. An application module template from the Erlang mode for Emacs

```
%%%-------------------------------------------------------------------
%%% @author $author
%%% @copyright (C) $year, $company
%%% @doc
%%%
%%% @end
%%% Created : $fulldate
%%%-------------------------------------------------------------------
-module($basename).

-behaviour(application).

%% Application callbacks
-export([start/2, stop/1]).

%%%===================================================================
%%% Application callbacks
%%%===================================================================

%%--------------------------------------------------------------------
%% @private
%% @doc
%% This function is called whenever an application is started using
%% application:start/[1,2], and should start the processes of the
%% application. If the application is structured according to the OTP
%% design principles as a supervision tree, this means starting the
%% top supervisor of the tree.
```

```
%%
%% @spec start(StartType, StartArgs) -> {ok, Pid} |
%%                                      {ok, Pid, State} |
%%                                      {error, Reason}
%%      StartType = normal | {takeover, Node} | {failover, Node}
%%      StartArgs = term()
%% @end
%%--------------------------------------------------------------------
start(_StartType, _StartArgs) ->
    case 'TopSupervisor':start_link() of
        {ok, Pid} ->
            {ok, Pid};
        Error ->
            Error
            end.


%%--------------------------------------------------------------------
%% @private
%% @doc
%% This function is called whenever an application has stopped. It
%% is intended to be the opposite of Module:start/2 and should do
%% any necessary cleaning up. The return value is ignored.
%%
%% @spec stop(State) -> void()
%% @end
%%--------------------------------------------------------------------
stop(_State) ->
ok.


%%%===================================================================
%%% Internal functions
%%%===================================================================
```

Index

D

data storage, alternative approaches to, 171
data types, for documentation/analysis, 182
data, structured (see structured data)
database management system (DBMS) (see Mnesia)
debugging
    through a GUI, 114-121
    tracing messages, 121-123
    watching function calls, 123
declarations, record, 127
DETS, 142
Dialyzer, 171
disk-based storage (see Mnesia)
distributed computing, 170
documentation, 18-24
    application, 23-24
    data types for, 182
    functions, 21-23
    modules, 19
duplicate bags, 133

E

EDoc, 19-24
Elixir, xi, 172
empty lists, 68, 69
Erlang (generally)
    calling functions, 5
    community, 172
    compilation and runtime system, 15
    etudes/exercises for, ix
    installation, 1
    languages built on, 172
    learning resources, x
    numbers in, 6
    operators, 177
    reserved words, 176
    shell, 2-4
    shell commands, 175
    starting, 2
    syntax, xii
    tools for connecting with other programming languages, 172
    working with variables in shell, 8-10
Erlang runtime system (ERTS), 15
Erlang Term Storage (ETS), 132-143
    creating and populating a table, 134-139
    overwriting values, 140
    simple queries, 139
    storing records in, 132-143
    tables and processes, 140-142
errors
    debugging through a GUI, 114-121
    flavors of, 109
    logging progress and failure, 113
    processes and, 95
    raising exceptions with throw, 112
    tracing messages, 121-123
error_logger module, 113
etudes, Erlang, ix
exceptions, raising with throw, 112
exercises, Erlang, ix
exit trapping, 104

F

F#, xi
f() function, 10
factorials, calculating, 47-51
filtering list values, 81
flattening lists, 66
floating-point numbers, 6
folding lists, 83-85
fun
    as keyword for defined function, 16
    creating functions with, 11-13
function calls, watching, 123
function clauses, 26, 30
functions
    and case construct, 37-40
    and variable scope, 16
    calling, 5
    creating with fun tool, 11-13
    defining in compiled modules, 13-18
    documenting, 21-23
    higher-order (see higher-order functions)
    if construct, 40-42
    io:format, 43
    list of, 179
    logic inside of, 37-43
    reserved words and, 176
    running list values through, 80
    simple recursion, 44-51
    tracing, 123
    using records in, 130-132
    watching calls, 123

G

generator, 80

About the Author

Simon St.Laurent is a content manager at LinkedIn Learning, focusing primarily on frontend web technologies. His interest in the server side, and experience chairing the Open Source Convention (OSCON) made him think that Erlang approaches would be the future on the server. He's authored or coauthored books including *Introducing Elixir*, *Introducing Erlang*, *Learning Rails 3*, *XML Pocket Reference*, 3rd Edition, *XML: A Primer*, and *Cookies*.

Colophon

The giant red flying squirrel (*Petaurista petaurista*) ranges from Afghanistan to Indonesia, and is most frequently found in the forests of Pakistan. It lives in the trees, and can glide between them thanks to the membranes of muscle and skin between its front and rear legs. These nocturnal creatures are most active in the early evening, feeding on pine cones, leaves, branches, and sometimes fruit, nuts, and insects. Average squirrels have a body approximately 16 inches long plus a slightly longer tail, and weigh almost four pounds.

Many of the animals on O'Reilly covers are endangered; all of them are important to the world. To learn more about how you can help, go to *animals.oreilly.com*.

The cover image is from *Wood's Animate Creation*. The cover fonts are URW Typewriter and Guardian Sans. The text font is Adobe Minion Pro; the heading font is Adobe Myriad Condensed; and the code font is Dalton Maag's Ubuntu Mono.

Learn from experts.
Find the answers you need.

Sign up for a **10-day free trial** to get **unlimited access** to all of the content on Safari, including Learning Paths, interactive tutorials, and curated playlists that draw from thousands of ebooks and training videos on a wide range of topics, including data, design, DevOps, management, business—and much more.

Start your free trial at:
oreilly.com/safari

(No credit card required.)

Milton Keynes UK
Ingram Content Group UK Ltd.
UKHW051832270924
448907UK00006B/101